families
on foot

families on foot

Urban Hikes to Backyard Treks and National Park Adventures

JENNIFER PHARR DAVIS AND BREW DAVIS

FALCON®

Guilford, Connecticut

An imprint of Globe Pequot
Falcon, FalconGuides, and Make Adventure Your Story are registered trademarks of Rowman & Littlefield.

Distributed by NATIONAL BOOK NETWORK

British Library Cataloguing in Publication Information available

Library of Congress Cataloging-in-Publication Data available

ISBN 978-1-4930-2671-5 (paperback)
ISBN 978-1-4930-2672-2 (e-book)

∞™ The paper used in this publication meets the minimum requirements of American National Standard for Information Sciences—Permanence of Paper for Printed Library Materials, ANSI/NISO Z39.48—1992.

Printed in the United States of America

We'd like to dedicate this book to family young and old: our daughter Charley, who's shared many adventures with us; son Gus, with whom we'll share many more; and grandparents Charlie Brewer and Adelaide Davis, who passed away just before this book was written. Pawpaw and Muno, someday we'll all share in the Greatest Adventure together.

contents

Preface

Call it walking. Call it hiking. Just get up and walk. Seldom has something so much fun also turned out to be so good for us. For American Hiking Society, the characteristics of hiking include walking recreationally and walking in a natural environment (and, yes, trees and plants in the city count!). Everyone can be a hiker. Whether you walk for fun or fitness, to watch the leaves change on the trees, or maybe to notice the birds among the plants, you're hiking—no matter where that hike takes place—on dirt or paved trails. Find a nearby trail and take a hike to experience the natural wonders of a city park or backcountry wilderness.

With numerous trails in and near urban and suburban centers, getting out on the trail has never been easier. Whether the trail is a converted railway line, a dirt path in the park, or a walk in the woods, family hiking close to home is an easy way to up the fun level of physical fitness. American Hiking Society believes that families that hike are healthier and happier. We created the *Families on Foot* initiative to: 1) reconnect children and families with nature, while making hiking and outdoor recreation an enhanced part of family life in America; 2) help families find the path to healthier living through increased physical, outdoor activity; and 3) build a growing nationwide voice to promote family hiking and advocate for support of family-friendly hiking and trail opportunities for all.

Hiking is a terrific way for families to spend time together. It is a fun, cost-effective outdoor activity that can improve individual health and well-being as well as family communications across all generations. And while it may seem too good to be true, the Centers for Disease Control and Prevention states that just 150 minutes a week of moderate-intensity aerobic activity, such as brisk walking or hiking—or 75 minutes a week of vigorous-intensity activity, such as

hiking uphill or with a heavy back-pack—provides significant health benefits. Hiking can lower the risk of heart disease and stroke, type 2 diabetes, high blood pressure, colon and breast cancer, and child-hood and adult obesity. And getting fit and healthy by hiking is not about expensive workout clothes, running, or going to the gym—just get the family together and enjoy a brisk walk. Simply put, when both adults and children hike, they not only reap the health benefits of hiking, but the fact that it's an enjoyable recreational activity keeps them coming back. That consistency is what sets hikers up for a lifetime of physical fitness.

Hiking the trails near Sedona, Arizona
DAVIS FAMILY

Trails with even a few trees or a little greenery around them bestow numerous mental health benefits. Specifically, time spent walking in nature is associated with reducing depression as well as with improvements in memory and a reduction in anxiety. Time spent in natural settings also alleviates symptoms in children of attention deficit/hyperactivity disorder. Such findings indicate that one need not travel to a remote national park to reap the benefits associated with being in nature, but rather that hiking trails with foliage along one or both sides may be sufficient. This means that every family—wherever you live—has some "nearby nature" to hike to and experience.

Jennifer Pharr Davis and Brew Davis serve as American Hiking Society's Family Ambassadors and provide simple, ready-to-use information suitable for families of any type and fitness level. Follow Jen and Brew's advice to find a local trail, make a plan, and hike your own hike.

Whether it's a hike in the park or a walk in the woods, hiking is a fun and affordable nature-based outdoor activity that will lead everyone in the family to a lifetime of fitness. And here's a feel-good moment: The younger our children are exposed to hiking and the outdoors, the greater chance we have of enabling the next generation to be environmentally aware, connected with nature, and on the path to lifelong health. What greater legacy can we leave as parents?

From my family to yours, happy hiking!

Gregory A. Miller, PhD
President
American Hiking Society

Jackson Hole, Wyoming
MP (MEGAN PETERSON) PHOTOGRAPHY

Introduction

As parents who love spending time on the trail with our friends, family, and—most importantly—our young daughter, we truly believe that hiking is one of the best activities you can engage in with your partner and your brood. It's an inexpensive hobby that you and your family can start with simply a pair of sneakers, a raincoat, and a basic first-aid kit.

Hiking is really accessible; it can literally be done just about anywhere by anyone. Choose from thousands of trails across the country (and the world)—be it an urban path, a simple wooded trail through a state or local park, or a back-country excursion. And the good news is that even if you identify yourself as a novice hiker, you're really much further along than you think. We *Homo sapiens* have been doing this hiking thing for tens of thousands of years—it's in our DNA. No matter how much experience you have as a hiker, you have loads of experience as a *walker*, and, as we like to say, "Hiking is really just walking in the woods, so how hard can it be?"

That comment is a bit tongue in cheek. As easy and fun as hiking can be, you aren't hiking in a vacuum. You hike with your family, and obviously being out in the woods with a brood of kids will present challenges. Your newborn might have a diaper blowout on the trail and, oops, you

Charley, Jennifer, and
Brew Davis doing
what they love best
DAVIS FAMILY

forgot the wipes. Your middle school son might cut his knee climbing on a rock beside the trail. And there's a chance—just a *slight* chance—that your teenage daughter will want to race through a hike because she'd rather be lying on her bed at home texting her friends. Your kids may complain about the bugs. Or if there are no bugs, they may complain about the wind or the light rain that's keeping the bugs at bay. It could be too hot—or too cold; too cloudy, too sunny, or even too beautiful. You get the picture.

If you think of your family hiking adventure as a tree, this book is the seed. We cannot anticipate every single challenge that the tree could face as it grows. But if you plant the seed and take care of it, that tree will grow strong roots, and those roots will allow the tree to flourish despite the challenges it will face.

So bring on the diaper blowouts—we'll show you how to tackle the messes while out on the trail. And don't fret over that cut knee—we'll give you plenty of safety tips for how to pack for and act on that very scenario. And as for that teenage daughter glued to her cell phone? We'll share some tricks that will get her looking up and around, engaged in the natural world around her. In just ten chapters we'll show you how to prep for the trail, enjoy the hike, and engage in some much-needed family time in the woods.

WHO WE ARE

Full disclosure: As the parents of an amazing, vivacious 3-year-old named Charley, we've yet to face the challenges that many of you have faced with your older kids. But we've hiked tens of thousands of miles across the country and the world, we've written quite a few books, and we've seen a *lot* of scenarios through our work with different age groups—Brew as a middle and high school teacher for seven years (he started hiking programs in both settings) and Jen as a camp counselor for ten years with every manner and age of young people. We also learned a ton from hiking in all fifty states with Charley before she was 2, and the diversity of those hikes—the weather, the landscape, and a host of other environmental factors—gave us a strong sense of the challenges families face in every corner of the United States, from the Florida Everglades to Wrangell–St. Elias National Park & Preserve in Alaska, from Hawai'i Volcanoes National Park to the remote mountains and lakes of central Maine.

Since 2008 we have owned and managed Blue Ridge Hiking Company in Asheville, North Carolina. Our company's vision statement is "The trail is there for everyone at every phase of life." Whether a couple wants to take a day hike with their infant, a group of deaf hikers want to hike to 100-foot waterfalls, or some senior adults are considering an extended overnight trip on the Appalachian Trail, we pride ourselves on making the wilderness accessible and enjoyable to everyone.

The one takeaway that has stayed with us through every adventure, and the one thought we want to leave you with as you start digging through this book, is this:

It's worth it!

Spending an afternoon making homemade granola with your 6-year-old is worth it. Schlepping that diaper bag to the top of the mountain is worth it. Turning around before the summit because your 12-year-old has blisters is worth it. Whatever it is, it's worth it, because you're spending *focused* time together—in nature—as a family. And what's more important than that?

MP (MEGAN PETERSON) PHOTOGRAPHY

Follow the Path

In 2011 Jen wanted to see how quickly she could hike the Appalachian Trail. I had a two-month break from teaching, and with being a mom waiting in the near future, Jen knew her days of traveling light and fast would soon be floating away like dandelion seeds in the wind. Speed-hiking the Appalachian Trail seemed appealing.

When Jen finished her hike, she got all sorts of questions about numbers—the number of calories she'd consumed, the number of hours she'd hiked each day, the number of miles she'd covered after dark. But for her it was a lot less about the numbers than it was about the memories made, the lessons learned, the relationships formed with the people in the support crew. Those are the things that lasted long after the hike.

the nuts and bolts of hiking

American Hiking Society

This book covers the nuts and bolts of hiking in a fairly in-depth manner. But this is a book about hiking with your family, right? So right about now your third grader is probably asking you for help with his math homework or your eighth grader needs a ride to her band practice. To ensure that you don't walk away from this first reading empty-handed, here's a crash course on hiking with your family from our good friends at American Hiking Society. If you have follow-up questions, rest assured we'll discuss everything at length later on.

If you're a hiker with young children, you don't have to put your hobby on hold until they head for college. And if you're a parent who is new to hiking, there couldn't be a better time to start. Spending time on the trail offers a world of opportunity for family outings and vacations. Not only will your family grow closer, but you can introduce the next generation to all that trails offer for personal growth and education while creating lifelong family memories.

When hiking with children, the trek no longer becomes about getting from point A to point B but more about exploring the trail and what's on it. With that in mind, here are a few thoughts to help keep your hike kid-friendly:

Have fun and be flexible. If this is your number-one goal, everyone will be happy. Remember that you're trying to introduce your family to hiking; they won't want to do it again if they don't have fun the first time. Change your plans if things are not working out.

Give the kids some control. Let the kids set the pace, and allow them to make some choices along the way. Let them decide which trail to take or where to stop for lunch. They will naturally want to explore their surroundings and examine new bugs, spiderwebs, and birds. You could carry a few toys for younger kids to play with if they seem to get distracted. Better yet, see if they can invent their own playthings using only objects they find on the trail, like rocks, sticks, leaves, etc. Just make sure to put it all back when you leave.

Bring snacks and plenty of fluids. Make sure to stop and drink frequently. Kids may be so interested in their new environment that they don't realize how thirsty they are. High-energy foods and plenty of water will keep them in good spirits.

Dress yourself and your children in layers. Be aware of your child's body temperature. If you are carrying a child, he or she may be cold while you are burning up. Conversely, you may feel chilled while your child is warm from running around and playing. If you have several kids, especially ones who may want to run ahead, dress them in bright, visible clothing so that you can more easily spot them.

Pick a short, interesting hike and allow lots of time. Choose a trail with a destination such as an overlook, waterfall, historic site, stream, or lake. Allow them time to investigate interesting things along the way. To start, choose a place close to home so your children don't get restless on a long drive.

Jen and Charley in the Narrows, Zion National Park
DAVIS FAMILY

Teach, sing, and play games with your kids. Discuss how long the trail is, trail etiquette, signs of impending weather, how to use a compass and read a map, and how to identify plants and animals.

Safety first. Give each of your kids a small pack with a healthy snack in it as well as a kid-size water bottle. They may also be old enough to carry their own jacket in the pack. Importantly, put a safety whistle in each pack. (If the kids don't have their own pack, attach the whistle to a zipper pull on their clothes.) Before each hike, review with the kids what to do if they should become separated from you. Ensure that they know to stay put and blow their whistle in three sharp bursts. Sometimes kids "get it" better if they're told to use the whistle to "find Mom or Dad" rather than "if you get lost," since they might not understand what being "lost" means.

And it's our hope that those will be the things that last for you and your family as you strike out on the trail together.

Listen, we know life is busy and that there are a dozen reasons "today's just not going to work out" for a hike. But if you make it a priority to get your family on the trail, we promise that you will see amazing results.

We've seen our daughter's curiosity piqued on a trail in a manner that simply can't be replicated indoors. We've had fascinating conversations with our parents and siblings that we never would have started—or had time to finish—without a long dirt path. And we have grown closer as a family because of—not in spite of—the hardships and the frustrations the trail presents. Our hope and our belief is that hiking will be one of the best things you ever do with your family.

STILL NEED CONVINCING TO STEP ON THE TRAIL?

We know how busy it is with family. You're pulled in dozens of directions at any given time—work at the office, school for the kids, meals to cook, chores and errands to check off the list, on and on it goes. You may think, "We have so much on our plates already. We love the idea of hiking, but can we really justify carving time out of our crazy schedules to just go for a *walk*?"

Well, friend, that's a great question. And unlucky for us, we don't know you and your situation well enough to answer it for you. But we *do* know about hiking, and we've seen firsthand the infinite benefits of doing it as a family. So we'll do our best to provide you with a veritable mountain of reasons you should prioritize time on the trail with your loved ones. We're confident that at the end of this section, you'll agree with us.

Practical Benefits

Hiking is beginner-friendly. Compared to other outdoor sports, the learning curve is minimal, and it's also much easier to involve young children and do with your entire family. Plus, in a world filled with competitive sports, it's nice to engage in an activity where you're not performing or comparing yourself to others. You'll see us reference HYOH a lot in this book—that stands for Hike Your Own Hike—and it's a popular acronym in the hiking community. On the trail you're your greatest competition, and the challenge is always going to be your own personal limitations.

Hiking is incredibly accessible and inclusive. There are literally hundreds of thousands of miles of trail crisscrossing the country, and the vast majority of them are free and open to the public, which means no annual membership, no registration fee, and no automatic renewal policy. Isn't that great news? In the twenty-first century there are still some things you can do for free!

What's more, no matter where you live—big city, small town, or suburb; East Coast, West Coast, or Third Coast—there is bound to be a hiking trail within a 30-minute drive of you. And the trails are as diverse and unique as the citizenry of our great nation.

Charley Davis plays on an Alaskan trail.
DAVIS FAMILY

Hiking is all about getting outside and walking in nature. You can hike around a farm, on a greenway, or down a beach. If you can't find a city, state, or national park in your region, search for a national forest or wildlife management area. Did you know that the Appalachian Trail is less than an hour's train ride from the middle of Manhattan? Or that Los Angeles has the world's first "urban trail"? It's called the Inman Trail, and it's 300 miles long.

Most states either have long-distance footpaths or are developing one—the Buckeye Trail in Ohio, the Foothills Trail in South Carolina, the Arizona Trail, the Superior Hiking Trail in Minnesota, the Centennial Trail in South Dakota, the Ouachita Trail in Arkansas and Oklahoma. We could go on. If you still come up empty, ask a local outdoor store or hiking enthusiast to point you in the right direction. Trust us; hikers love to share their knowledge of local trails.

We devote an entire chapter to gear, but while we're on the topic of affordability and accessibility, we want you to know that if you have snacks in your pantry, Band-Aids in your medicine cabinet, a comfortable pair of walking shoes, and a set of workout clothes, you and your family have everything you need to take your first day hike. And it won't hurt our feelings one bit if you set this book down right now and walk out the door. Go ahead. We'll see you in a few hours. . . .

How was it? Fun, right? We told you.

Mental and Physical Benefits

Let's play a quick word association game. If we asked you to associate the phrase "9 hours" with your teens, what would pop into your head? The amount of time they spend sleeping at night? The length of their school day? Or, if they are *really* dedicated, maybe the number of hours spent practicing a sport, musical instrument, or something else? How about this? In fall 2015 a nonprofit called Common Sense Media released a report that said the average teen in the United States spends 9 hours on media every day—TV, Internet, movies, music, video games, and social media. Nine hours! That's amazing—and appalling.

Needless to say, hiking helps disconnect your kids from all that technology. We're sure this fact is reason enough to go out on the trail for a lot of you parents reading this book. But there are plenty of other reasons to get your kids outside, so let us count the ways.

Mental health. Scientists have recently released a theory called Attention Restoration Theory, or ART. They assert that replacing time in the office or classroom with time outside can increase attention spans and problem-solving skills by up to 50 percent. And researchers from Stanford's Graduate School of Education have found that walking lends itself to creativity far more than sitting does. Do you see where we're going with this?

Time Spent Outdoors + Walking = Hiking = More Creativity and Focus.

Beyond that, nature is the ultimate classroom. It poses riddles for the scientist and mathematician; it inspires the author, the artist, the composer; and it begs questions and reveals truths for the historian. Regardless the discipline, nature inspires the creative and rewards the curious. And don't we all need a little more creativity and curiosity in our lives?

Physical health. The physical benefits are even more obvious and plentiful than the mental ones. And they're all the more important since our school systems are cutting back on recess and Physical Education while childhood obesity has doubled in the past thirty years. For starters, hiking builds strong bones and muscles. And it's not just strengthening your legs; it's a total body workout that incorporates everything from your feet and ankles to your shoulders and neck. Hiking also strengthens your heart and your lungs. It reduces the chances of you or your children becoming overweight (hiking burns up to 500 calories an hour), and it lowers health risks for high cholesterol, high blood pressure, type 2 diabetes, heart disease, stroke, breast cancer, colon cancer, and early death. It even reduces stress levels and depression. Especially helpful for parents, it can improve your children's quality of sleep at night. And as all parents know, the better a child sleeps, the better the parents sleep too.

Did we mention we love hiking?
DAVIS FAMILY

Emotional Benefits

The emotional benefits of hiking are just as important as the mental and physical, especially for young people. And in many ways they go hand in hand (no pun intended). Getting on a trail distances them from the societal pressures and mass media marketing that are so prevalent today, replacing them—literally and figuratively—with a breath of fresh air. And when in that setting, good things are bound to happen. Regardless of whether you view the connection between humans and nature as spiritual, biological, or both, it's undeniable that some sort of connection exists.

When we ponder nature and the interplay between us and it, we can't help but be stirred internally. Putting your daughter in front of a powerful waterfall, a breathtaking view, or the quietude of a meadow at dusk could lead to an emotional awakening or a better understanding of her place in the world. Or it could allow her to process a relocation or loss of a loved one or friend. If she's struggling with a class or the fact that she got cut from the JV basketball team, climbing a mountain could provide the physical challenge that boosts her self-esteem. Cleaning up a polluted watershed could give her a feeling of empowerment and seeing the "before" and "after" could lead to an "aha" moment: "Hey, I really *can* make a difference."

And with those internal benefits come external ones as well. Specifically, hiking strengthens bonds with the land and with loved ones. Volunteering on a regional work crew or hiking through a local mountain range can give your son a stronger sense of place and a closer relationship with home. (What parent doesn't want his or her kids to stay closer to home when they grow up?)

Besides creating a love of local landscape, hiking creates a love of *all* landscapes and a desire to conserve and protect natural resources. When your daughter plays in a creek or hikes in a rainstorm, she'll make connections between your local watershed and the water she drinks from your kitchen sink. When a trail is rerouted because of a wildfire or because campers didn't practice Leave No Trace principles, your son sees firsthand the impact that humans have on the environment. When he discovers that one of his favorite animals is endangered due to urban sprawl, he'll think about sustainability and responsible land development.

real story

Walking the Distance

Our family planned a sabbatical year at Grand Canyon National Park, and we knew our 5- and 7-year-old daughters, Amy and Molly, would love it. We'd walked and hiked with our girls from the very beginning. They started by riding in a backpack then graduated to walking around the neighborhood and to the store with us and doing weekend family hikes. Walking was just a natural thing for all of us to do.

So after all that walking practice, we finally found ourselves at the Grand Canyon, and the Colorado River at the bottom of the canyon was beckoning. We planned our hike carefully: 7 miles and nearly 5,000 feet of descent down the South Kaibab Trail to Bright Angel Creek, two nights in the bunkhouse, and then 10 miles and more than 4,000 feet of ascent up the Bright Angel Trail. We started our hikes very early each day to avoid most of the afternoon heat, and we carried lots of water and snacks. We used a modified Hansel and Gretel approach, dealing out hard candies and other rewards to Amy and Molly as we passed important landmarks.

The Manning family heads down through the Grand Canyon toward the Colorado River.
MARTHA MANNING

Our practice paid off. The girls did great, walking every step of the way and having a blast exploring this dramatic landscape, so different from our native Vermont. (Mom and Dad did okay too.) Our daughters drew a lot of attention at the bottom of the canyon—it's rare to see such young children doing what is commonly perceived as a demanding hike. The girls were obviously pleased with themselves, and justifiably so. The year was memorable for all of us, and our hiking adventures were especially important. Some of our daughters' fondest childhood memories revolve around these hikes.

Our daughters are women now, and they are still hiking. Each has converted her urban husband as well, all of them doing long-distance hiking. And now we have two grandsons who join the fun. Hiking is important to our family. Aside from being great exercise, it strengthens family bonds and offers a human-scale approach to appreciating the iconic landscapes of the world. Start children walking early in life so they take it for granted that walking is natural and enjoyable, and pass along the joys of walking from one generation to the next.

—Robert and Martha Manning, authors of *Walking Distance: Extraordinary Hikes for Ordinary People*

It's hard for children—and adults, for that matter—to fully appreciate something until they've experienced it. If they don't appreciate it, they won't want to protect it. And if they don't protect it, it won't be around for future generations. America's National Park Service marked its one-hundredth anniversary in 2016. What a wonderful milestone! But state and national parks, as well as the forests, wilderness areas, and recreation areas protected by city, state, and federal governments, are facing serious budgetary cuts, not to mention enormous pressure from land developers and energy companies. Taking your children outdoors is one way to foster the next generation of conservationists, environmental stewards, and conscientious global citizens. If we want our national parks to be healthy when they reach their 150th, 200th, or 500th anniversaries, we're going to have to work at it. And one way to start is simply to take a hike.

But let's bring it back to a more personal level, to you and your family. In an era where we all get pulled in different directions, hiking together removes you from those distractions and strengthens your family ties. It's different from going to a movie together, coaching a Little League team, or helping

a child with a science project. Those are all great things, important things. And studies have shown that the amount of time children spend with their parents doing literally anything can positively impact academic performance and reduce the risk of behavioral problems and substance abuse. But those activities don't offer the focused attention that hiking provides.

Remember the movie *Field of Dreams*? The climax comes when Kevin Costner's character, Ray Kinsella, who has plowed over his corn and built a baseball field for the chance to spend a little extra time with his late father, says simply, "Hey, Dad . . . want to have a catch?" There's a lot of symbolism in a father and son throwing a baseball back and forth—the connection, the conversation, the give-and-take. And there's just as much symbolism in a parent leading a child down a stretch of singletrack or walking together side by side on a greenway or gravel road. In a world of busy-ness and noise, words don't even have to be spoken; time together can be enough.

One Final Reason

Did we mention that we *love* hiking? We love hiking as individuals and as a couple. But most of all we love hiking as a family because it combines our two favorite things: hiking and one another. It also happens to be something we can do together for the rest of our lives.

As for you, dear reader, we'd like to think that you already love your family, whatever the word "family" means to you. It's our hope that after reading this book, you'll love hiking as much as we do—and that you'll want to share it with your family for the rest of your lives.

There's nothing better than finding your "happy place."
DAVIS FAMILY

Jackson Hole, Wyoming
MP (MEGAN PETERSON) PHOTOGRAPHY

chapter 1

Make a Game Plan

When our daughter, Charley, was an infant, I found it difficult to get on the trail because we were operating within 3-hour feeding windows. By the time I got my pack ready, threw in some extra diapers, picked a hike, and mapped out the driving directions, it was once again time to feed Charley and put her down for a nap. We missed our chance to get out the door because we weren't prepared. Over time, I've learned that the best way to get my family outdoors is to make the planning and preparation as easy and stress-free as possible.

So now the first thing I do to get my family on the trail is keep a fully stocked daypack in our front hall closet. We also keep a large bowl filled with local trail maps and hiking pamphlets next to the guidebooks on our bookshelf. Sometimes when I can't decide where to go, I'll let Charley dig her hands into the hike bowl and pick a map at random. She loves doing this because, even now at age 3, she feels she has some control over our outing. And 3-year-olds love control!

In all my experience hiking and backpacking with children, I've come to find that the hard part actually happens *off-trail*. Once you are out in nature, the hike, the environment, and the activities tend to keep everyone engaged and having fun.

Planning for a hike doesn't just require physical preparation; emotional and mental preparation are equally important. I have led quite a few trips over the years, and without fail at least a handful of the group members show signs of panic in our pre-hike briefings. They ask questions like "What if I have to use the bathroom on the hike?" "Are there snakes out there?" "Will there be cell service?" But once we actually start hiking, the entire group is laughing and singing, and the anxious ones have forgotten their troubles.

Trekking through Spain
KAREN RIDDLE

Most teens come to recognize that time on the trail is a break from their regimented routine. There is no pressure in the woods because nature does not care about grades, extracurricular activities, or the prom. They forget that their cell phones are on "airplane mode." We almost never see a snake, and when we do they think it's "sweet." And by the end of the outing, more than a few of them take pride in the fact that they peed in the woods for the first time.

Being properly prepared and overcoming fears and inexperience might be the hardest part of taking a hike. But that doesn't mean there won't be mishaps on the trail. Anytime you go out, there's the risk of spraining an ankle, getting a blister or two, or getting rained on. But it's important to remember that there's magic in the mishaps.

One time I was out with Charley when it started to rain. It was the first time we had been caught in a downpour on a hike, and I immediately felt like a horrible mother. As I rushed to the nearest trailhead, I heard Charley making a funny noise. Initially I thought she was fussing over her first encounter with a rainstorm. But when I looked down at her in the Babybjörn, I saw a giant smile stretching across her face and a look of wonder in her eyes. She was laughing and having a ball; she hadn't yet been conditioned that rain was something to avoid.

Charley taught me an important lesson that day about letting go of control in the outdoors. Sure we take precautions and pack appropriately, but ultimately we go outside because we want to feel the rain on our cheeks.

This chapter is aimed at helping you feel comfortable and competent when you hit the trails with your kids. Like any other new skill, hiking has a learning curve. Try your best to incorporate your family into the entire process from start to finish. This not only gives them ownership over the experience but also instills in them the skills and knowledge they can use to be safe and have fun outdoors as they grow older. You can't know it all on your first hike. In fact, you won't know it all on your last hike. Just do your best to *plan* out your hike, *prepare* everyone mentally and physically, and *pack* appropriately ("the P's of hiking")—and then be willing to learn as you go.

—*Jennifer Pharr Davis*

Ah, fall!
DAVIS FAMILY

OH, THE PLACES YOU'LL GO: RESEARCH AND PLANNING

It is a great time to be a hiker. There are trails everywhere, hiking gear has significantly improved in the past few decades, and the resources for getting your family outside are more abundant than ever. Nowadays, if you have a question about hiking, you don't have to look far to find the answer. Between guidebooks, online tutorials, and local workshops, it's easy to learn more about how and where to hike.

So where do you begin when you're planning a family outing? Guidebooks are a great starting place to learn general information about an area and find trails near you. The benefit of a guidebook is that it's a condensed, backpack-friendly source with almost everything you need to know within its pages. Use it to plan your hike at home, and then take it with you on the trail. Treat your guidebook like your personal travelogue. Write notes in the margins, dog-ear important information, or highlight your favorite routes to come back to time and again.

If it's published by a credible outdoor press, have confidence that the information in the book is as accurate as possible. Typically, guidebooks are more trustworthy than what you find online. But because trails frequently change due to maintenance, reroutes, and detours in the area, and because books still require some time to get out new editions and updates, many publishers offer a place to post online updates to their guides; be sure to check those for any pertinent updates for the guidebooks you use.

A hat, water bottle, map, and compass are always a good idea, no matter how experienced you are.
ANDREW LAHART

Trail Tech

Map My Hike

You may have heard of the popular fitness tools "Map My Run" and "Map My Ride," but did you know that the same company offers a website and phone app called "Map My Hike"? This interactive tool searches for hiking routes that have been uploaded by others. Users not only share their favorite hikes but also leave notes and updates on trail conditions. Map My Hike provides a plethora of information during your outing. It tracks your route using the built-in GPS and also tells you the distance traveled, your pace, elevation gain and loss, and more. You can even input your trail snacks and compare your caloric intake with the number of calories you burn on your hike. Challenge friends to set and compare hiking goals, or you can join a Map My Hike group for added encouragement and motivation. Best of all, the app allows you to share your routes and stats on social media so you can help other families discover all the great trails in your area. With Map My Hike, you become the author of your own hiking guide.

Not all web-based trail tidbits are accurate, but you *can* find factual, helpful information on the Internet. There are some terrific online trail resources out there. Our buddy Andrew Skurka offers loads of advice on his website (andrewskurka.com), and you can find hike options at sites like alltrails.com, trails.com, and rootsrated.com. When you find a blog or hike description you like, cross-reference it with other sources for accuracy.

If searching online for helpful information about hiking, start by visiting American Hiking Society's website: americanhiking.org. This organization is dedicated to promoting and protecting trails throughout the United States, and the website includes helpful trail tips and inspirational, informative blogs.

If you are a visual learner, then search tutorial videos on YouTube or other video-sharing sites. You can gain a lot of tips and techniques through hiking videos posted online—everything from how to hang a bear bag on overnight trips to how to identify spring wildflowers and even information about local trails in your area.

Regardless of where you go to find information, purchase and pack a map for your outing. A map is the most basic resource you can have on the trail and provides alternative trails for unexpected occasions. Trails, guidebooks, and online materials can and will change, but for the most part, mountains and rivers are constant. If you learn how to read a topographic map—at a workshop, by using a guidebook, or through an online tutorial—then you are setting yourself up for a safe and successful trip.

Baby Steps: Begin in Your Own Backyard

One of the best things about hiking is that you literally take it one step at a time. You don't have to scale Mount Kilimanjaro or traverse the Appalachian Trail on your first hike—or on any hike. Plenty of fulfillment and joy can be gleaned from taking your family on short local hikes. It will make the wilderness feel accessible to your family, giving them a sense of place while also teaching them about your local ecosystem.

Begin in your own backyard. Take your kids for a walk around the neighborhood and talk with them about the different things you see. Point out the flowers, trees, and birds, but be sure also to mention the houses, cars, streets, and other man-made items. These brief excursions give your family some basic walking experience, but more importantly they provide a framework for comparison when you spend time in a more natural setting. They also provide teachable moments for you to discuss the importance of wild places and allow you time to ask your children what they might expect to see on a wilderness adventure as opposed to a walk close to home. Teachable moments come in all sizes and forms, whether it's stopping to point out a bee pollinating a flower or crouching down to place your little one's footprint inside the larger track of a wild animal. It's important to slow down and take the time to look around—any number of teachable moments are just within your eyes' view. They will leave lasting impressions on your kids for years to come and help them learn about the wildlife outside their doors.

Proper planning beforehand ensures you'll be all smiles on the trail.
KRISTOFFER ISRAEL

Once you are comfortable walking around the block as a family, research local parks that offer family-friendly nature trails. Contact your local parks and rec department or nature preserve to see if they have any upcoming guided hikes. Participating in group outings with a park ranger or outdoor educator is a great way for you and your children to improve your hiking skills while acquiring fun and useful knowledge from an expert. If you're going unguided, these trails often are marked with kiosks and signposts that help you identify plants and learn more about the local ecosystem. If you are a true novice hiker, you might consider inviting a more experienced friend to join you on your nature walk and point out fun features along the way. And don't worry if you're unsure of where to look; chapter 10 is dedicated entirely to helping you track down trails using online resources, local trail clubs, etc.

Expanding Your Hike Area

Once you become comfortable and competent hiking in your backyard, your city, and your county, you can expand your reach to state parks, national parks, and national forests. Build a solid foundation now, and get more adventurous later on. Learning the basics of hiking will open up a world of adventure for you and your family.

FIND A BUDDY: HIKING GROUPS AND ORGANIZATIONS

Typically, the most enjoyable way to learn about hiking is not in an armchair or behind a computer but in person. Countless hiking workshops and outings are available to the public, and many of them are free or low cost. For example, American Hiking Society sponsors National Trails Day on the first Saturday in June. Each year on this day, AHS partners with local trail management agencies, outfitters, and hiking groups to offer hundreds of free trail events across the United States. You can join up with your local park or hiking group for this nationwide event, which is a great way to enjoy and celebrate outdoor recreation and trails with thousands of other Americans. It is also a wonderful opportunity to discover local trail clubs and hiking activities in your neck of the woods.

Go Local

Your local outdoor store may also offer up a hiking group or workshop. Some national retailers like REI and Bass Pro Shops have ongoing community events to engage and inform the public. The topics of these classes range from outdoor skills to inspirational stories, backcountry ethics to local trail information.

If you're a new parent looking for a hiking companion, consider asking Grandma to go with you.
RITA FOX

Typically these larger stores list community events on their website, where you can register online.

Local and independent outdoor stores also host quality programming for their patrons. Check the local business listing for independent retailers, or search the Grassroots Outdoor Alliance by visiting grassroots outdoors.com. Call the store directly to ask about upcoming programs, or check the business's social media sites. Small businesses often use platforms such as Facebook to publicize events.

Reach out to nearby parks and preserves to see if they offer any ranger-led workshops. These classes are taught by rangers or outdoor educators who are familiar with local flora, fauna, and trails. Events held during the week are a great opportunity for families who homeschool their children. Sometimes during the summer months, parks and other natural areas offer a series of learning opportunities or hikes for the entire family. This is a great opportunity for children of all ages to learn in an

Trail Mix

Preparing for a hike doesn't have to focus solely on research, planning, and organization. Sometimes the pre-trip activities at home are almost as fun as getting on the trail. Preparing healthy snacks for your family to enjoy during your outing is a great way to get ready for your hike. Here is a simple recipe for making granola bars at home—and even the littlest members of the family can help.

©THINKSTOCK.COM/SSTAJIC

Nutty Chocolate Granola Bars

2 cups rolled oats

½ cup shredded coconut

½ cup chocolate chips

½ cup peanuts

Dash of salt

2 tablespoons peanut butter

2 tablespoons Nutella

¼ cup honey (or maple syrup)

Optional: If you like your granola bars a little fruity, consider throwing in some dried cranberries or banana chips. Like them extra nutty? Include a handful of almonds or pecans.

1. Preheat the oven to 325°F then grease a 9-inch baking dish. Use butter for the tastiest results.

2. Combine the oats, shredded coconut, chocolate chips, peanuts, salt, and any additional dried fruits or nuts into a large mixing bowl. Stir the ingredients together. Remember: Little helpers love to stir!

3. Put the peanut butter, Nutella, and honey in a microwave-safe dish and heat for 30 seconds. Nuking it will reduce the viscosity of all the thick, gooey ingredients—and will also give you time to teach everyone the meaning of "viscosity."

4. Add the peanut butter, Nutella, and honey mixture to the dry ingredients and stir thoroughly. It should get harder and harder to combine as the ingredients cool, so use those muscles.

5. When the mixture is consistent, spread it evenly into the greased baking pan and put in the oven for 10 minutes.

Let the granola bars cool for 15 minutes before cutting them and tasting the results. Don't forget to save a few for the trail!

Leave No Trace

You might hear "Leave No Trace" referenced throughout this book (see chapter 7 for more information). Leave No Trace means to leave nature as you found it. Basic Leave No Trace principles include not littering, not picking flowers or plants, and packing any bathroom tissue or trash out to the nearest trailhead. Besides being good for the planet, being a good steward of the environment can also help keep you and your family safe. How? When your group stays on the trail, it reduces the human impact on nature, cuts back on encounters with ticks and poison ivy, and keeps the group from potential unseen hazards, such as cliffs.

outdoor environment that can complement the curriculum presented in a traditional classroom setting.

Meet Up Online

More and more informal hiking groups and naturalist clubs are forming and promoting their offerings online. Online "meet-up" groups have become a popular way to meet like-minded individuals with similar outdoor interests. Search for hiking meet-up groups in your area by visiting meetup.com. Or check out parent-specific resources like hikeitbaby.com. These online meet-ups and social groups are a great way to hit the trails and connect with people, but a word of caution: There's no guarantee that a trip leader will be an expert hiker or that a member of the group will be trained in wilderness medicine and be carrying a first-aid kit. So be sure to plan and pack accordingly when you participate in any organized trip.

Hire a Professional

If you really want to learn from an experienced hiker and are interested in moving your backyard exploration to more organized wilderness areas, it might be worth the time and money to hire a professional guide. Joining a commercial group hike or securing a personal trip leader is like paying any other private coach for a lesson—you will likely be learning from a skilled practitioner who is certified and credentialed in some way. Most hiking guides are either trained in wilderness first-aid or certified as a wilderness first responder or wilderness emergency medical technician (EMT). Guiding companies typically provide food and gear on outings, so you don't have to worry about planning meals or buying an item you may only use once. Although they're often costly, another advantage of hiring a professional guide is that the outfitter or individual will most likely be able to customize a trail experience to meet your needs and schedule.

Join a Trail Club

Perhaps the best way to experience some hiking while also giving back to the trail community is to search for a local trail maintenance club. Many of these clubs are located near national long-distance trails such as the Appalachian Trail, the Colorado Trail, the Pacific Crest Trail, and Vermont's Long Trail. The

Appalachian Trail is actually maintained by volunteers who are organized into thirty different trail clubs stretching from Georgia to Maine.

Plan before you go—about where you're going to go and what you expect from the hike.
DAVIS FAMILY

Most trail clubs are very affordable to join and offer a range of hikes and trail maintenance projects. They connect you with a community of outdoor-minded people in the area, and membership usually comes with freebies to help you begin your hiking adventures. Many trail club members are retired and have more time to devote to weekly outings than do families with young children. However, the trail clubs typically embrace and celebrate younger members, and they often provide family-specific outings and age-appropriate challenges designed to help children learn about the natural world. Children who complete these challenges are often rewarded with a club patch or certificate, deepening their connection to the trail community.

WHERE'S WALDO? ESTABLISH COMMUNICATION BEFORE YOU HIKE

Before you even step foot on the trail, always let someone know where you're going and when you plan to be back. If there is a register at the trailhead, sign in and include your group size and intended destination. And let everyone in your group know that you need to stick together. In general, it's important to communicate clearly with everyone in the group about the hike and your expectations for it. With family, this usually means differentiating information to make sure kids of all ages—as well as adults, frankly—are on the same page.

If you're a parent you probably do this intuitively, but just to provide a trail example, if you're trying to convey to a 5-year-old that he needs to stay put if he gets turned around on the trail, get down on his level, look him in the eyes, and say, "If you don't see one of us, I don't want you to panic. Just stay where you are, make some noise, and we'll find you. Don't move around, because that could make it harder for us to find you. Do you understand?" If, on the other hand, you're hiking with middle school kids, remind them that the woods are not an appropriate place to play hide-and-seek.

Clear communication before the hike is essential, but keeping the dialogue open while on the trail is equally important. If someone is uncomfortable, tired, or hungry at the start of the hike, it will most likely get worse as the outing progresses so have frequent check-ins with your group to gauge feelings. Is anyone hot? Tired? Hungry? Regardless of age, all hikers need

reminders to eat and drink frequently, use the restroom before heading out, and take frequent breaks along the path. This allows slower hikers to rest and regain their energy without feeling like they're holding up the group. If you sense a family member becoming self-conscious about his or her pace (especially an elementary school kid trying to keep up with her buddies), make the breaks less obvious by stopping to take more pictures or pulling out a guide and identifying the flowers along the trail with the group.

EMBRACE YOUR NATURAL SKILLS

It is impossible to ever be fully prepared for any hike. Unexpected things happen. You might encounter wildlife on the trail. Or, if you hike after a heavy rain, what was once a trickling spring may have morphed into an impassible wall of water. You could start hiking in the mountains on a beautiful summer afternoon under bluebird skies only to find yourself being pelted by marble-size hail from an electrical storm 2 hours later. Or you might take a winter hike—fully prepared and well dressed—only to have a serious problem on your hands when your son or daughter loses a mitten.

But breathe easy. Some of the most important hiking skills are not necessarily taught but rather are innate within all of us. Instincts and fear can help keep you safe. Practice common sense, keep calm, and use creative problem solving to help you avoid disaster.

real story

Hiking Tips for Large Families

My wife and I fell in love with hiking before we were married and brought the children into the woods at the earliest opportunity. Our five kids have grown up on the trail. Of course, they'd sometimes rather be home playing Minecraft or visiting with friends. But they will never forget these moments of togetherness. And they learn valuable skills, like how to encourage a group without leaving people behind. The trail life also shows kids that the wild side of nature is fun, not scary.

On our best days, we plan ahead and pack the night before. The older kids pack their own bags with water bottles and snacks. Footwear is the most important equipment. Children's waterproof hiking boots are fairly inexpensive and worth the money. Happy feet can help people overcome a lot of discomforts. Extra care is required with smaller kids and cold weather. Their extremities get cold much faster than ours. Handheld radios are good if your children are spaced apart in age like ours are. The older ones don't have to hike at a 4-year-old's pace as long as we can still contact them on the radio.

It's fun to watch the kids grow up on the trail. The smaller ones are enthralled by sticks and rocks and usually keep a collection with them while they hike. As they get older, they recognize plants and animals they've learned about in school and create their own trail adventures. Sometimes the kids hike alongside Mom and Dad and chat about life.

We like to scout out a good resting place and have lunch on the trail—nuts, cheese, fruit, granola bars, crackers, chocolate—whatever seems like a good idea that day. Sometimes we cook hot dogs. These long stops give everyone a chance to recuperate and take in the space around them.

In recent months I've been battling cancer. Treatment has made hikes more difficult. But I've found that I cherish these hikes even more now. The trail helps me feel normal again and gives me strength. There are so many parallels between hiking and life. I can face challenges in the perspective of life's journey. I don't know what's over the top of that next rise. But if I keep pressing on, the view at the top will be well worth the trouble.

—Greg Reddin

Overlooking Arkansas—the Reddin family on the trail
GREG REDDIN

LEARN FROM YOUR FEARS

You do not need to overcome all your fears to start hiking. In many cases, natural fear and adrenaline provide you with a healthy respect for and reaction to, say, a potentially dangerous animal or a lofty precipice. For example, if you come around a turn and run into a hundred-foot cliff, a positive response is to stop, stay calm, and slowly back away. Your instinct is heightened in the woods to help you avoid or escape danger. Listen to it. Don't let fear hold you back from hiking; rather, use it to keep you and your family safe on the trail.

Practice Common Sense

Common sense is also key to a successful family outing. For example, keep weather in mind when planning for and taking a hike. If the water at a stream crossing is higher than usual and you have any doubt about crossing it successfully, look up- and downstream for a safe place to ford; if you don't see a safe crossing, turn back. You can always return to complete the trail when it's drier. And when you make these commonsense decisions, always consider everyone in the group and weigh their enthusiasm and comfort level.

©ISTOCK.COM/MONKEYBUSINESSIMAGES

Perhaps you arrive at a stream crossing and you have a slight hesitation about whether your crew can wade through it. Your 7-year-old daughter is confident that she can cross safely and is already sticking her toes in the water, but your usually talkative 5-year-old looks terrified and isn't saying a word. Always strive to make the best *group* decision possible, and don't weigh one person's desires—including your own—more than someone else's discomfort. In this way, the trail is a great place to practice making decisions as a family.

Find Your Inner Zen

The ability to stay calm is important on any trail, but it's especially so when you hike with children. Children, like the weather, can be very unpredictable. Even if you start hiking on a perfect summer day in a sunny place like Southern California where the weather remains fairly consistent, conditions can still change very quickly. If you are at high elevation and see storm clouds gathering, tell your family in a composed manner that the weather doesn't look so good and it might be time to head back down the mountain. Use your inner Zen to keep the group calm, keeping them on pace but not rushed or running down the mountain, which could cause panic and would certainly increase the risk of someone falling on the trail.

Be Creative in Problem Solving

Creative problem solving skills are also essential to a safe and successful family outing. It is amazing what children and adults accidentally lose or leave behind on hikes. Your toddler might fall asleep in a kid carrier on your back and lose a shoe. Your 6-year-old might leave behind her water bottle after a snack break during a desert hike. Your middle schooler might realize that he has misplaced his mitten after throwing too many snowballs at his sister. A lost mitten on a winter hike might be grounds for heading back to the trailhead, but there is a chance you can improvise another hand warmer so that you don't have to cut the hike short. For example, an extra wool sock could be placed over chilly fingers and used as a mitten. Or if someone is wearing a hat but also has a hood on his or her jacket, the beanie could be wrapped around the exposed hand, potentially secured with a rubber band or hair tie. Assuming the hand is warm and has strong circulation, your hike can continue as planned.

Research and plan as well as possible prior to hitting the trail, but don't feel like you have to know it all before you start. There isn't a single person out there who knows *everything* about hiking; you can always learn more hiking skills and techniques. But as long as you keep exploring different trails in different places with family members of different ages, you will increase your knowledge. And remember, some of the best skills and know-how for the forest are already part of your parenting and relational skills. Knowledge and preparation can get you out on the trail safely, but ultimately instincts, common sense, level-headedness, and creative problem solving will make your hike a success.

next step

So you have a few family day hikes under your belt and want to take your outdoor experience to the next step? Perhaps you want to camp out or backpack in a wilderness area a little ways away from home? Here is a checklist for next steps you can take to get there:

1. Prepare in the backyard.
   - ☐ Borrow camping gear to test equipment before you buy it.
   - ☐ Let children bring comfort items into the tent. Make bedtime transition easier by doing all teeth brushing and pajama prep inside before camping outside.
   - ☐ Try a backyard campout with friends.
   - ☐ Follow your kid's lead; if he gets spooked in the middle of the night, bail on the tent for the comfort of the bed inside.

2. Move on to car camping.
   - ☐ For the first car camping experience, try a nearby campground.
   - ☐ Experiment with the campground facilities—like the coin-operated showers.

3. Advance to tent camping.
   - ☐ Don't go too far from the trailhead for your first overnight in a tent.
   - ☐ Let children bring a special comfort item from home.
   - ☐ Be aware of your children's feelings, and take your cues from them.

chapter 2

Safety on the Trail

L ast winter I hiked with Charley just a few weeks after undergoing knee surgery. I had the "all clear" from my doctor, and I was *itching* to get back on the trail. So I put Charley in the kid carrier, hoisted her on my back, and headed down a rocky path beside a creek. It was early March; the mountain air was cold and brisk, and a heavy rain that morning made the trail wet and slick. After walking for close to an hour, not yet at our predetermined turnaround point, my knee started to hurt. So for perhaps the first time in my life, I decided *not* to test my limits. Instead I turned around and made my way safely, albeit gingerly, back toward the car.

These days, I spend a lot more time thinking about trail safety. I was never reckless in days past, but now I'm constantly thinking not only about how to keep Brew and Charley safe when we're together but also about how to keep myself safe when I'm hiking alone, whether I'm out for the day or for a week or two. I know that when Charley and I go hiking by ourselves, she won't be able to care for me if I get injured. If I want to keep her safe, I know I have to keep myself safe too.

So back to that early March hike with Charley. She slept in the pack for the first half of the hike, but once I turned around she woke up and started fidgeting in her carrier. And every time she flung her weight in one direction or the other, I felt my balance shift on that surgically repaired knee. I focused on my foot placement and began to regret picking such a dicey trail to tackle my first time out.

My pace slowed to a near crawl. It was late in the afternoon; the sun had started its descent, and with it the temperature dropped too. Charley was cold and bored, so she did what any baby in her position would do—she fussed. I stopped to put on her winter jacket, hat, and mittens and put her back in her

Boise River
©THINKSTOCK.COM/
BENTLEYPHOTOS

When out on the trail, be aware of the distinct risks your family may face.
DAVIS FAMILY

pack. She wasn't happy about being confined again, but we didn't have time for her to meander on the wet trail if we were to get to the trailhead before dark. I had a headlamp in the pack, but it was a small consolation. I knew that night-hiking on slippery rocks with a fidgeting kid on my back and a gimpy knee would be dangerous.

We made it back to the car just before the sun set; I couldn't have been more relieved. In retrospect, I am glad I made the decision to turn around early rather than continue on. But I also should have chosen a smoother path with fewer rocks and roots. After that hair-raising experience, I started asking Brew or one of our friends to join me on upcoming outings, at least until I was fully recovered.

—Jennifer Pharr Davis

ASSESSING SAFETY AND RISK

Because we manage a hiking company, we probably think more about trail safety and risk management than most folks do. We provide outings for all ages and ability levels, so our guides are aware of the distinct risks that face the different demographics of children, adults, and seniors. We have an exhaustive manual dedicated to keeping our guides informed and our clients safe. You might think it reads like a Bear Grylls manual or one of those *Worst Case Scenario* books. But actually the most prevalent risks we encounter on hiking and backpacking trips are not specific to the trail. Instead they are encounters with unfriendly off-leash dogs and food- and insect-related allergies. The same holds true for our personal outings with Charley.

Jen saw a black bear on one of her first hikes with Charley, and she's been alone with Charley in remote settings on numerous occasions where other large mammals lurk. But the only time either of us ever felt truly in danger while carrying our kiddo was when a loose dog jumped on Jen and knocked her down.

Sure you should always steer clear when you see bears and other wildlife, but in reality it is the seemingly mundane things that bring the most risk on the trail. While fairy tales and the Internet have us wary of big, nasty woodland creatures, the truth is that the biggest risks and concerns you have for your family on-trail are often the same ones you find off-trail.

So don't fret all that much about the "what-ifs"; instead, simply be prepared. Remember, if you can clean and bandage a scraped knee at home, you can handle it on a hike. If you can administer Benadryl and epinephrine for an allergic reaction in your backyard, you can do it in the woods too. You already have most of the basic know-how you need to keep your family safe outdoors. This chapter provides a handful of on-trail first-aid skills you may not have considered.

BE PREPARED: GENERAL AT-HOME PLANNING FOR YOUR HIKE

Be prepared. Isn't that what the Boy Scouts say? Well it's true for anyone who intends to spend time in the wilderness. The best way to hike safely *on* the trail is to prepare well *off* it.

The first way to ensure the safest hike possible is to plan your trip wisely. Consider your hike's

A Programming Note

This section covers several universal tips for staying healthy and injury-free, and the sections that follow offer a few age-specific thoughts on safety. However, this chapter should serve only as an introduction for keeping your family safe. The tips and advice listed here can be expanded on with additional research and training. There are a number of books devoted specifically to hiking safety, as well as online resources and personal classes that can enhance your knowledge of first aid in the backcountry.

geographic location: What state is it in? Are you familiar with the terrain? Will you have shade in a forest or be exposed to sun all day? Are you hiking through a meadow or above tree line in the mountains?

Next, consider the season in which you're hiking: What's the weather forecast? Will it be hot or cold, wet or dry? How much rainfall has there been recently, and how might this affect water sources? The first time or two you go out, brainstorm these questions and consider any variables with your kids. The more experience you have in the woods, the more these considerations become second nature (no pun intended).

Doctor, Doctor, Gimme the News: Fill Your First-Aid Kit

Always take a first-aid kit with you. While this is true in all scenarios, it is especially true if you're hiking in a more remote location. Your kit will be prepared based on your family's specific needs. There are countless options that vary depending on the duration of your trip and the level of wilderness medicine training you've received. Start with a small basic first-aid kit filled with bandages, tape, triple antibiotic ointment, and calamine lotion.

From there, customize the kit by talking to your general practitioner and family pediatrician. Tell him or her where you plan to go and how many miles you hope to cover. Discuss preexisting conditions and ask questions about how best to treat them on the trail. Your doctor can suggest age-appropriate over-the-counter medicine for everyone. And depending on your family's medical history, he or she may also write prescriptions to treat such things as poison oak or bee stings.

One other thing you should add to your wilderness first-aid kit checklist is your cell phone. Having a *charged* cell phone can save your life in an emergency.

Trail Tech

American Red Cross App

One fabulous tool worth downloading before you take a hike is the American Red Cross app, which has organized potential health risks into categories. With the touch of a finger you can find lifesaving information on allergies, asthma, broken bones, burns, head injuries, heat stroke, hypothermia—the list goes on. Being in an atypical setting can challenge the focus of even the best-trained medical professionals, but having industry standards at your disposal can help you stay calm and administer treatment even when you're forced to improvise. The app can also help dispel common myths. For example, some old movies and TV shows portray scenes where one person has been bitten by a snake and another applies a tourniquet then sucks the venom out with his mouth. The app will instruct you not to do this (not even you, Rambo) and will give you the proper steps to follow instead. One important reminder when administering first aid: Don't try advanced lifesaving techniques if you haven't been properly trained in them. In other words, stay within your pay grade even when on the trail.

Allergies

Food, insect, and environmental allergies (such as pollen or animal dander) are a concern on the trail just as they are off it. Hikers with known allergies should consult with their doctors to determine whether they need to carry epinephrine. At a minimum, the first-aid kit should be stocked with an antihistamine such as Benadryl; don't forget to pack the children's version too.

Allergens shouldn't be a deterrent to getting out on the trail. However, there is a *chance* you could come in contact with something out there that you have not been exposed to before, and this is especially true with children. If someone in your group is, say, stung by a bee for the first time on a hike, you should monitor them closely for signs of an impending allergic reaction. Sometimes even rubbing up against a specific plant can be enough to cause a reaction. If you notice symptoms of an allergic reaction—itchiness, watery eyes, swelling, hives, or difficulty breathing—first ask him what he thinks is causing it. Perhaps he ate something out of the ordinary, brushed up against a tree, or was bitten by an insect.

> **A Programming Note**
>
> *The information and legality concerning epinephrine changes constantly and is regulated state by state (and there's been much debate recently about the potentially prohibitive costs of EpiPens), so it's a good idea to consult with a doctor on when and how to administer it. It's also important to ask how to handle the individual after he's received the medication.*

If you *know* the person is not allergic to antihistamines, the best way to treat and prevent allergic reactions and anaphylaxis (severe, life-threatening allergic reactions)—whether to a known or unknown substance—is to administer the drug as soon as the individual shows symptoms. You'll want to pack enough for the entire group, since the lead hiker may stir up a beehive or yellow jacket nest, resulting in stings for everyone who comes after her.

After that, you'll have to make a judgment call about whether to let the person rest or evacuate him. Either way, you and the others should do everything you can to keep the affected hiker calm and comfortable.

Finalize the Number of Hikers on the Trip

When hiking with your family, you may stick together or split up. When larger groups hike, they tend to expand and contract on the trail like an accordion, sometimes splitting up into two or three smaller groups. And that's okay. Just be sure to discuss the expectations with everyone *before* you start, determining a safe range and demonstrating that to your group. Be sure you have a good adults-to-kids ratio on the hike, have a responsible adult within eyesight of every child, and get into the practice of calling everyone back together before you get too far down the trail.

When we hike with school groups or other families, we always have one adult at the front of the pack and another bringing up the rear. Elementary- and middle school–age kids have a tendency to run ahead, so remind them they are *not* the line leader—and that if they break ranks there will be no milk and cookies when they get home, or s'mores around the campfire. Encourage the leader of the pack to stop at any trail junction or stream crossing so that the rest of the group can catch up. This way if—heaven forbid—someone does wander off-trail, you'll have a better idea of when and where he or she went missing.

Before you head out, go over what needs to happen should anyone get separated from the group. There is of course a lower risk of having this happen if you hike together. Still, you should remind everyone—including adults—that if they think they're lost or can't see the group, they should *stay put and call out for help.* If they have a cell phone on them, they can try to ring someone. If they are carrying a whistle, they can blow it three times to signal to the rest of the family.

If you find yourself lost *as a group*, the most important thing to do is stay calm. In fact, when we get turned around in the woods, the first thing we do is take a snack break. This mellows us out and gives us time to check our map and guidebook rather than make a knee-jerk decision.

If you're confident of the way you came, retrace your steps to a trail marker or unique feature (for example, an oddly shaped tree or a rock outcropping). If you can't find your way back to the correct path, check for GPS or cell signal on your phone. Perhaps you can pinpoint your location on a map. Call out loudly and see if any other hikers respond. If you get no response, try to place a call—you'd be surprised at the amount of cell coverage there is these days, even in the wilderness.

So this is what a trail blaze looks like!
PETER DARGATZ

"If lost . . . stay put and call out for help."

If you don't have any bars, try to call out anyway; your failed attempt can hit another provider's tower and provide a rough idea of your location and the time you called. Calls have a better chance of getting through if you're at a higher elevation. And if you move around a ridge or out of a hollow, you may establish a connection that was previously out of reach.

If you've exhausted all your options and haven't gotten anywhere, make yourself as comfortable as possible and settle in. Yell out occasionally, and stay in one place to make it easier for park rangers, other hikers, or the search-and-rescue (SAR) team to find you. The chances of your getting rescued are infinitely higher if you're near a trail—*any* trail, even if it's not the trail you meant to be on—than if you start bushwhacking through the underbrush.

Lions and Tigers and Bears, Oh My: Wildlife

As with getting lost or separated, plan *before* you hit the trail what you'll do if you encounter animals. And here's a good rule of thumb to start with: Leave wildlife alone. Remember that animals like bears, snakes, and mountain lions are usually just as scared of you as you are of them, and for that reason they'll avoid you. But if you do encounter wildlife on a family outing, give the animal as much space as possible. Stop and wait for it to move off into the forest, or keep moving to put more distance between you and the animal. With any potentially dangerous creature, though, you should try not to make any sudden moves.

Marmot
DAVIS FAMILY

While many new hikers worry about encounters with larger animals or venomous ones, *all* wildlife (skunks, porcupines, moose, foxes, deer, elk, beavers—the list goes on) should be left alone and given a wide berth. Generally speaking, if you hit the trail at midday and make a lot of noise, as groups tend to do, chances are you won't have any unexpected run-ins. Of course, if you *want* to catch sight of some critters, your best bet is to hike when they are most active—typically dawn and dusk—and to stay relatively quiet. Having an animal encounter on the trail can startle you and cause a rush of adrenaline, but it can also be an incredibly memorable experience for you and your children. In fact, most of our favorite moments in the woods have been when we spotted a bald eagle, a moose, some bear cubs digging up grubs under a stump, or even a rattlesnake sunning itself on the trail—all viewed from a safe distance of course.

Ticks

In certain areas of the country, ticks are a huge concern for hikers. In the mid-Atlantic, for example, deer ticks and the Lyme disease they sometimes carry have had a major impact on outdoor recreationalists. Hiking in winter is one way to decrease your chance of being bitten. A second is to wear long sleeves and long pants, even in summer. Bug repellent containing DEET is another effective measure. Permethrin can be used to treat clothing and gear, but you shouldn't apply it directly to your skin. If a tick comes in contact with a sock, shirt, even a tent that has been treated with permethrin, it's a goner.

More and more, natural remedies are being developed that repel ticks without the use of artificial ingredients. No matter which prevention method you chose, you should frequently check for ticks on yourself and the rest of your family. Since deer ticks are tiny, they can often be mistaken for a freckle or small mole so it's smart to search for ticks with your hands as much as your eyes. You may not always be able to see a tick, but you can almost always feel one.

Ticks have to be embedded for over 24 hours to transmit Lyme disease. If you find a tick that has dug into your skin, remove it with tweezers, getting as close to the head as possible. If a red circle develops around the bite or you start to feel sick, call your doctor immediately and describe the bite and the symptoms.

While deer ticks transmit Lyme disease, larger dog ticks can pass along Rocky Mountain spotted fever, though it's much less common. It is important to be aware of all ticks and to be vigilant on hikes, but with new technology and products, there are also more ways to keep them from ruining your trip.

Lightning, Severe Storms, and Extreme Weather

A negative or even life-threatening experience in the elements can often be prevented by taking a few minutes to study the forecast *before* you leave for a family hike and to pack accordingly with extra layers or items for protection. Still, there are times when storms can develop quickly and catch you off guard.

If an electrical storm approaches out of nowhere, get to a lower elevation quickly but safely, find terrain that is not exposed, and, if possible, take cover in a building such as a wooden trail shelter or ranger station. Don't hide out in fire towers, and avoid other tall, metallic structures. If there are no buildings nearby when it starts to storm, you can set up a tent or tarp and huddle inside on your packs or on a sleeping pad. If you do not have a shelter or pad, then make sure your family members put on their warmest layers and their rain gear. Find the safest place possible (ideally in the forest), spread out within eyesight of one another, and then squat down.

Weather rolling in
ELLA CLARKE

If you are carrying a thin daypack or anything with insulation, stand on it to create at least a modest buffer. When your feet are touching the ground, they can conduct energy from a nearby lightning strike to your body, so you want to create as much separation between you and the earth as possible. Next, squat with your hands behind your neck. This is called the "lightning position." It's not very comfortable, and you'll need to stretch out every now and then, but it's the best way to keep you and your family safe.

If you're hiking high in the mountains, be aware that the temperature can drop very quickly; you can experience hail, sleet, or even a snowstorm in the summer months. Pack extra layers, and keep an eye on your children for signs of hyperthermia if you're out for a prolonged period. A moderate hike will be more taxing on a child than on most adults, and if your kids are not dressed appropriately or are not eating or drinking enough, their body temperatures can drop quickly. If that happens, get them warm by giving them extra layers and food, and then descend to a safer, warmer environment as soon as possible.

Extreme heat can also be a cause for concern on family hikes. On sweltering, humid days, remind everyone to drink *and* eat enough. This will prevent dehydration and also hyponatremia, which is a lack of sodium in the bloodstream. If you are taking a trek with older parents or grandparents, take frequent breaks and stay cool to prevent heat stroke. If someone seems overheated, get water in the person. And if you have a ready supply of it or if you're near a creek or lake, get water *on* the person as well.

AGE-SPECIFIC TRAIL PREPARATIONS AND SAFETY

Let's face it—wrangling a toddler on the trail can be *a lot* different than trying to get your teenager to look up from his phone long enough to take in majestic nature-scapes. Since your experiences can vary drastically depending on the age of your children, the following section offers some age-specific preparations and safety tips to keep in mind so that the entire family enjoys its trip in the woods.

Send In the Cavalry

When planning your trip, you can't always predict emergencies. But you should always have a general plan of what to do if you encounter one. If you have a serious or life-threatening situation, call for help immediately. If you don't have cell service, send two people to call for help. Communicate details (like location and the patient's conditions) as clearly as possible. This information will be very helpful and may increase the efficiency of search-and-rescue efforts to locate you and provide assistance.

While we're aware of how "worst case" parts of this chapter can read, it's only because we've had to condense a lot of safety issues into a handful of paragraphs. But just remember—there is nothing inherently dangerous about walking in the woods. In fact, our daughter has had far more cuts and bruises from toddling down the sidewalk than wobbling down the trail, even though she spends roughly the same amount of time on both. And it sure is nice not having to worry about traffic for a while.

Preschool and Younger

Taking a baby on the trail can be a blast. They're lightweight and portable, which is terrific for hiking. And unlike older kids, you don't have to worry about them running ahead, lagging behind, or poking big brother's nose with a stick.

There's a good chance your infant will absolutely *love* your time together outdoors, and that means *you'll* love your time outdoors too. Take a fussy baby on a hike, and he may actually stop crying for a bit. Better yet, the rhythm and repetition of your footfall can be so soothing that he falls asleep altogether and doesn't wake up until you're finished. Woohoo! Talk about a win-win situation. From a safety standpoint, taking an infant or toddler out can be much easier than

Dad and Fairy at Zion
DAVIS FAMILY

When hiking with younger kids, keep one adult up front and the other at the rear.
SUE EISAGUIRRE

taking older children, primarily because they're either riding on your back the entire time or within a few feet of you.

For any young child getting a lift, you'll want to ensure that he's comfortable and that the kid pack isn't restricting his breathing in any way (we'll talk more about kid carriers in chapter 3). Up until 6 months of age, he'll most likely be carried in a front-facing carrier.

Whether you tote your child on your back or front, remember that his experience will be *very* different from yours. For example, he won't be working up a sweat or raising his body temperature as much as 6 or 7 degrees as you will, so it's important to dress him properly. No matter the season, you'll likely want to put him in long sleeves and pants to protect his skin from the sun or the cold. If it is hot and humid, make sure he's wearing lightweight, breathable fabrics. If it is cold, dress him in warm layers and add or take them away depending on his comfort level. And remember, when you start hiking your baby may shift or squirm in his pack; when he does his clothing can move around, so check every 15 to 20 minutes to make sure he's properly protected from the elements. In general, it's a good idea not to take extreme-weather hikes with young children or to keep them brief.

Be Careful with the Sunscreen and Sprays

The FDA recommends that you not use sunscreen or bug spray on babies under six months old because the chemicals are bad for their skin. After that, check with a doctor and read the warning label on any lotions or sprays before applying to your child's skin. And remember: These won't protect the infant from bee stings or insect bites, which is another reason to opt for long sleeves and pants.

I Like to Move It: When Your Toddler Wants to Walk

Oh, toddlers. Now's the time when children really start to get on the move, and what better way to let them stretch their legs than to go on a family hike? In this developmental stage, it can be fun to let him out of his pack and turn him loose. You may even find yourself making special trips to the trail because new walkers have a softer landing on leaves and dirt than on concrete and asphalt. But they're also more likely to take a spill among those pesky roots and rocks, so you'll probably want to lend them a hand at times. Long sleeves, long pants, and even gloves can be helpful to prevent kiddos from getting scraped up so easily.

As your child grows and begins to motor down the trail without assistance, make sure she stays on the path and avoids things like poison ivy and briar patches. Watch what she picks up, because bugs and potentially poisonous mushrooms and berries are just as likely to go into her mouth as Cheerios and fruit chews.

Charley off and running in the Rockies
DAVIS FAMILY

real story

Better Planning for the Trail

A couple of years ago, my husband and I took advantage of a rare unscheduled weekend by going hiking. A quick online search told us everything we needed to know. Our chosen destination, Fontana Dam and the nearby Appalachian Trail, was only a few hours away from our home. With all the planning complete, we tucked our four boys (ages 8 through 14) in bed early with promises of an early start and adventures at the end of a road known as Tail of the Dragon.

The next morning was beautiful, and we started off on our adventure almost on time. The trip to Fontana was uneventful, and we unpacked our supplies and headed off across the dam and onto the trail. In short order, we came to the trailhead and weighed our options.

We chose a trail that was approximately 3 miles long. Since we were a young family that did a lot of running, we reasoned that the 6-mile round-trip would be a walk in the park. We never imagined that a few miles in the woods could be so different than a few miles running the road. The attached photo was taken just before we reached the turnaround point. The boys were sure that we had gone at least 5 or 6 miles already and that we must have missed a sign. Perhaps the

Our "moment of doubt"—from left to right: Caleb, Eli, Ethan, and Micah Underdown
SARAH-ANN UNDERDOWN

incredulous looks a few well-equipped hikers gave to a family in shorts and sneakers might have sapped our collective energy.

Despite the mutinous spirit captured here, I rallied the boys—husband included—to finish what we started. We achieved our goal and returned to Fontana tired, hungry, and thirsty. After a long ride home and a quick tick check, we collapsed in our beds. It took us a few days to recover, but now we laugh about this experience often and try to plan better for future adventures.

—Sarah-Ann Underdown

And because infants, toddlers, and pre-schoolers can have their first run-in to allergens on the trail, make sure you have lotion and ointment for bug bites or plant encounters.

Elementary School

Most elementary school kids make terrific hikers. They're self-sufficient yet still obedient, and they're almost always up for an adventure. That said, there are definitely things you can do to enhance your child's trail experience while also keeping her safe.

First of all, don't model bad behavior, even in jest. Your young child is essentially a "Mini-Me" who will say and do whatever you do on the trail and off it. So don't jokingly hide from your spouse or pretend to eat a mushroom and keel over like a cartoon character, because your 7-year-old will likely do the same thing.

It can also be easy to overestimate your young child's skills and energy level. If you are hiking with older children, you still need to plan the trip with the youngest—and typically the slowest—child in mind. Trying to keep up with an older sibling can lead younger children into dangerous situations. Our good friend's daughter slid down a steep 15-foot embankment because she was trying to "beat" her brother down a flight of wooden stairs. Aside from some skinned elbows and knees, she was no worse for wear. But the lesson was clear: The trail is no place for a race.

Here's another example: Your teenager might not think twice about climbing a tree. But the distance between those limbs could be more of a stretch for your first grader, who may not realize she's gotten into trouble until she's 10 feet off the ground and smack in the middle of a real predicament. Always make sure your elementary-age child stays close to you, your significant other, or a responsible older sibling who fully understands the younger child's ability level.

Because this age group is so eager and enthusiastic about being outside, they might also have trouble with unfriendly—or excessively friendly—dogs. Remind them not to approach unknown pooches—*especially* if they're off-leash—until you have a chance to ask the owner if the dog is friendly and if it's okay to pet him.

Sometimes your kids will be fine on their own; sometimes you'll want to lend them a hand.
MP (MEGAN PETERSON) PHOTOGRAPHY

All too often, children approach dogs because they are used to well-behaved pets at home or in the neighborhood. But a domesticated animal *on* the trail tends to be a little friskier than it is in its normal setting. Even a friendly dog is more likely to jump on your young child and knock her over if he's been splashing in streams and chasing squirrels all afternoon.

When hiking with children under the age of 10, know all the access points on your hike. Here's where your early preparations at home really kick in. Hitting the trail with youngsters is unpredictable, so you may want to prepare a route in advance with different difficulty levels and choices for distance. For example, if you're doing an out-and-back hike (where you turn around at the farthest point), the best way to shorten it is simply to turn back earlier. But if you're making a loop or are in a confusing network of trails, it's best to keep your options open. Generally speaking, the more flexibility you have, the more everyone will enjoy the outing.

Oh, independence!
©THINKSTOCK.COM/PURESTOCK

We spoke briefly in the chapter overview about what to do if someone in the group gets lost. Since your infant or toddler will likely be on your back or within arm's reach, it's essential to reiterate to your youngsters—most likely around this elementary school age or whenever they start gaining a little more independence—what to do if they get lost. Let's refresh: Stay put and wait for someone to find you.

A tracker who had spent his career helping rangers find dozens, if not hundreds, of missing people in Great Smoky Mountains National Park recently shared the story of a 7-year-old boy who'd been separated from his mother on a short day hike. The tracker eventually found the boy hiding from the search-and-rescue team under a rhododendron bush because he thought they were bad men out to get him. Fortunately, this story didn't end in tragedy, but it's a cautionary tale that should really drive home the importance of teaching our children what to do if they get lost.

Middle School

Preteens usually bring a lot of energy to the trail, which means there are greater safety risks to be aware of when hiking with them. Contrary to today's popular preteen literature, though, vampires are not one of them. Neither are werewolves.

Middle school children want to be independent, so on the trail they will try to do as much as possible, regardless of whether they actually know what they're getting themselves into or whether you're supervising them. Keep this in mind when planning longer, multiday adventures more suitable to kids this age or older. And when teaching them backcountry skills or enlisting their help with camp chores, test their skills before you trust them to navigate. Or build a fire. Or cook. Or filter water. Or set up a tent. You get the picture. An ill-prepared or unsupervised helper is more likely to get injured by a stove, get sick from improperly treated water, or—worse—get *everyone* sick.

Middle school is also a time when kids are more self-aware. And self-awareness in nature can lead to discomfort and embarrassment. It is not uncommon for older kids or even adults to try their hardest not to pee or poop in the woods. Someone who does not want to "wilderness pee," as our daughter likes to say, usually tries to drink as little water as possible, which can of course lead to dehydration. Some may not want to go "number two" in the woods, but anyone who tries to refrain from pooping could end up with some major cramps and constipation.

Tread softly as a butterfly when your family's on the trail.
DAVIS FAMILY

Potty Time! (Not Party Time)

As the parent and group leader, discuss backcountry bathroom etiquette as soon as possible. Remind the group that there is no more perfect setting to take a whiz than a beautiful meadow, a mountain vista, or a nice, quiet grove of evergreens. Our instinct is to think that peeing or pooping on pine needles is less clean than a bathroom. But think about that for a second. Doesn't a public restroom—or even your own—have a hundred times more germs than an impromptu, never-been-used woodland latrine?

Do what you've got to do to convince your family that a forest bathroom break can actually be enjoyable. One way to facilitate the experience is to keep a "booboo" bag in your daypack filled with hand sanitizer, toilet paper, a trowel for digging holes, and any necessary feminine products. Speaking of hand sanitizer, this is another trail essential, since you may not always have access to water or soap.

Remember that most girls in this age group have started their periods. You will want to strike a balance between being supportive and helping deal with these issues without making them feel uncomfortable. No woman—young or old—should feel that she can't hike because she's menstruating. Handling it is similar to going to the bathroom in the woods. We'll discuss it more in chapter 7, in the Leave No Trace section. (Spoiler alert: Bring a plastic bag.) On the plus side, women who exercise during their periods typically have shorter, less noticeable ones. Share that with your daughter, mom!

Let teens explore solo or with friends to make the experience their own.
KRISTOFFER ISRAEL

High School

Hiking with older kids can mean covering more miles, but there are also increased risks when you're sharing the trail with someone who tries to exert his or her independence in all facets of life. Whereas preteens are only beginning to assert themselves, teens are in full-on "lone wolf" mode.

One of the best ways to foster a love for the outdoors in teenagers is to allow them to make the experience their own. Just be sure to point them in the right direction before sending them down the path by themselves. If you're having trouble keeping them engaged in the family experience, teach some basic first-aid skills. Play up the fact that this will give them greater independence for future adventures. And if they have any interest in becoming a doctor or nurse, wilderness medicine can be the perfect hook for coaxing them into the outdoors.

Although you might be hiking to unplug your child temporarily from social media, be realistic in your expectations of her use of technology. High schoolers will often want to document their outings so they can share them with friends online when they get home. Your teenagers may be content capturing photos of your happy little family sitting by the campfire, but it's more likely that they're going to want something *epic*, something Instagram-worthy.

So keep an eye on them—especially if your hike takes you past waterfalls or rock cliffs—and remind them to use their better judgment. We spend a lot of time with school groups. One minute we are soaking up a spectacular Blue Ridge mountainscape, and the next a pair of boys are 20 feet high in a tree. We should be used to it by now, but we almost hyperventilate every time.

This mindfulness is the same for wildlife sightings. Teenage boys seem particularly susceptible to lapses in judgment with regard to animals. In fact, most of the venomous snakebites we've heard about are a result of boys (sometimes grown men) teasing a rattlesnake or copperhead—even trying to grab one by the *tail*—without realizing how far those bad boys (the snakes, not the kids) can reach when they uncoil.

On the flip side, teenagers can be incredibly helpful in medical emergencies, being very strong hikers and having the potential to track down help quicker than younger children can. They're also further along developmentally and have the ability to problem solve and work their way out of serious predicaments if they can keep their cool.

We read recently about a Boy Scout troop of 12- and 13-year-olds in New Jersey who successfully rescued their troop leader after he'd been mauled by a bear. The boys stayed calm and did all the right things at critical junctures and because of it, their 50-year-old leader made it out alive.

next step

Interested in furthering your knowledge of wilderness medicine? Consider enrolling in a wilderness first aid (WFA) course. Open to individuals over 14 years old, WFA multiday workshops are held throughout the country and are hosted by reputable wilderness training institutes and field experts. The benefits are worth it:

- ☐ *They teach you the basics of assessing and treating injuries and illnesses in the backcountry and empower you to stay calm, cool, and collected in the face of an emergency.*
- ☐ *They also instruct you on how to protect yourself and others who are uninjured yet still in harm's way.*
- ☐ *Certifications look great on college applications, and they can be another entry point into hiking for your aspiring doctor or nurse.*
- ☐ *Many WFA classes include a CPR certification, which can save a life anywhere—not just on the trail.*

chapter 3

Purchasing and Packing Gear

Our good friend Warren Doyle is a trail addict. More specifically, Warren's an *Appalachian* Trail addict, having hiked the entire thing—all 2,189 miles of it—seventeen times. That's like walking around the equator one and a half times. Besides the sheer magnitude of those numbers, the most impressive thing about his hikes is that every one of them was completed on a shoestring budget. Rather than buy top-of-the-line equipment from specialty stores, Warren gets everything—headlamp, sleeping bag, you name it—at his local big box chain. He wears secondhand shoes from a thrift store and a single pair of socks for each hike (which is gross, but still very economical). And he uses a simple tarp instead of a high-end tent.

Now let's set the record straight: We're not against spending money on gear. We have an entire room full of it in our house. Having quality gear that works for you is essential for enjoying your time on the trail. Maybe you've heard the old Scandinavian saying, "There's no such thing as bad weather, only bad clothing." Well, that's just as true on the trail as it is in Norway, Denmark, or Sweden.

But the point of sharing Warren's unique approach is this: Unlike some other outdoor sports, you don't *have* to spend an arm and a leg to enjoy hiking. You just have to find the gear that's right for you. That gear may be expensive, but it can also be affordable or even downright cheap.

And while you may not need to spend wads of money to enjoy hiking, you do need to bring the right gear on each hike. One of my first trail experiences growing up in Tennessee was an overnight trip with some high school friends to Montgomery Bell State Park. It was the dead of winter, and the mummy bag I grabbed from the closet was the wrong one and at least 8 inches too short for me. Needless to say, that was one cold, miserable night.

Crater Lake National Park, Oregon
DAVIS FAMILY

I'm less likely to forget a tent or a sleeping pad than I am to forget a headlamp, a spork, or Vaseline to stave off skin irritation on a hot summer day. But to this day, when we go hiking I'm extra careful to pack even the smallest items. Having the right gear for your family is as essential to enjoying the trail as is being physically fit. It may take you a while to get those things dialed in, but just being conscious of them is a good place to start.

—Brew Davis

LEARNING FROM SANTA CLAUS: HOW TO PACK PROPERLY

When preparing your gear for a family hike, channel your inner Santa Claus. Make a list, check it twice, then stuff everything you need into a big sack and sling it over your shoulder.

If like us you have a young child, you're used to grabbing everything in sight—diapers, books, crayons, coloring paper, stuffed animals, a change of clothes. You name it, we've packed it. The gear changes as your child gets older, but the "grab and go" concept remains the same.

That said, carrying what your child needs on the trail is drastically different from carrying what he needs for a trip across town in the old minivan. The catch with the Santa Claus analogy is that you won't have any reindeer to help you tote everything, so you should only bring the gear you *need* and not everything you *want*. It's harder keeping up with everyone else, and you can't assist the kiddos as easily over technical terrain if you overpack on the trail. And if you have a little one, it is infinitely tougher to carry him for a few minutes if you're already struggling under the weight of an overstuffed pack.

Check your gear twice to make sure you don't leave anything out.
DAVIS FAMILY

To Each His (or Her) Own: Finding the Right Gear

Your gear needs will vary based on the age of your family members, but you don't have to spend thousands of dollars on fancy new equipment. Hand-me-downs are a great option. The carrier we used for the first year of Charley's life was a hand-me-down from our neighbors across the street, and the kid pack we used after that was a gift from a trail-running friend whose children had moved on to elementary school. In fact, most families are *thrilled* to get rid of the old equipment collecting dust in their garage or attic.

Look into purchasing slightly used gear online (Craigslist, anyone?), at a local thrift store, or at a second-hand sporting goods store. Loads of backpacks, tents, and sleeping bags that have been used only a handful of times are being sold for pennies on the dollar.

If your kids are already sporty, chances are last year's soccer jersey or basketball tank top will wick just as well as a new synthetic T-shirt. Your sixth grader's school pack will serve him just as well on the trail as in math class. And these days, it seems that every car dealership and business conference on earth gives out a free water bottle. So you don't have to spend a fortune to outfit your family. At some point you'll definitely want to invest in comfortable, quality gear, but it's worth waiting a bit to figure out exactly what that gear should be.

A Programming Note

The following sections are broken apart by school age ranges and offer age-specific gear. Feel free to flip ahead to the section that best matches your child's age to figure out how to fill your pack.

PRESCHOOL AND YOUNGER NEEDS

Young kids often aren't walking as much (or at all) on the trail as their older counterparts, so gear needs to be tailored to their special needs at this age. Here are a few unique gear items to consider for the younger hikers in the group.

Papoose (Part One): Finding the Right Baby Carrier

Unless you're walking on a greenway or a groomed trail, keep the stroller at home, even if you've got one of those sporty, expensive jogging strollers or an off-road one with big tires. You may be able to avoid the roots and rocks, but trails tend to have much steeper grades than the sidewalks and roads of most American cities. (San Francisco readers—ignore what we just said.)

It's important to have a comfortable baby carrier. Whatever you use at home also works on the trail for the first six to eight months of your baby's life. Popular brands include Babybjörn, Ergo, and Moby Wraps. Most models in the Babybjörn and Moby Wrap line only work if you carry your baby on your chest, but when he reaches a certain weight, that's no longer practical. So if you don't already have a carrier, consider an Ergo or

Cora and her kid carrier in snow—Wyoming
DAVIS FAMILY

The 10 Essentials of Hiking

Some gear is universal regardless of the different ages within your family unit. American Hiking Society has come up with a wonderful list of items you should include on every family outing. Drum roll, please . . .

1. Appropriate footwear. For a short day hike that doesn't involve a heavy pack or technical terrain, trail shoes are great. For longer hikes, carrying heavier loads, or more technical terrain, hiking boots offer more support.

2. Map and compass/GPS. A map and compass not only tell you where you are and how far you have to go, but they help you find campsites, water, and an emergency exit route in case of an accident. While GPS units are very useful, always carry a map and compass as a backup.

3. Extra water and a way to purify it. Without enough water, your body's muscles and organs simply can't perform as well. Consuming too little water will not only make you thirsty but also susceptible to hypothermia and altitude sickness.

4. Extra food. Any number of things could keep you out longer than expected: getting lost, enjoying time by a stream, an injury, or difficult terrain. Extra food helps keep up energy and morale.

5. Rain gear and extra clothing. Because the weatherman is not always right. Dressing in layers allows you to adjust to changing weather and activity levels. Two rules: Avoid cotton (it keeps moisture close to your skin), and always carry a hat.

6. Safety items: fire starter, light, and a whistle. The warmth of a fire and a hot drink can help prevent hypothermia. Fires are also a great way to signal for help if you get lost. If lost, the whistle is more effective than using your voice to call for help (use three short bursts). And just in case you're out later than planned, a flashlight/headlamp is a must-have item to combat the darkness.

7. First-aid kit. Prepackaged first-aid kits for hikers are available at any outfitter. Double your effectiveness with knowledge: Take a first-aid class with the American Red Cross or a wilderness first aid class.

8. Knife or multipurpose tool. These enable you to cut strips of cloth into bandages, remove splinters, fix broken eyeglasses, and perform a whole host of repairs on malfunctioning gear.

9. Sunscreen and sunglasses. Especially above tree line when there is a skin-scorching combination of sun and snow, you'll need sunglasses to prevent snow blindness and sunscreen to prevent sunburn.

10. Daypack/backpack. You'll want something you can carry comfortably and that has the features designed to keep you hiking smartly. Don't forget the rain cover; some packs come with one built in. Keep the other essentials in the pack, and you'll always be ready to hit the trail safely.

This list is a starting point, but you should personalize your hiking gear. Just be careful you don't overpack. Strike a balance between being comfortable while you're moving and comfortable while you're resting, especially on an overnight.

And what exactly do we mean by that? Well, if you really want a hot meal at night, by all means carry a stove. Or if you love reading when you're lying in your sleeping bag by the campfire, bring your favorite book. But just remember that your stove and book add a few extra ounces, and every extra ounce makes your time on foot a little bit tougher. In general, you'll know you have the right amount of stuff with you when you *use* and *enjoy* everything you carry.

If the weather's hot, wear lightweight clothing and cool off by a stream.
DAVIS FAMILY

a similar design that gives you flexibility to transition your child from your chest to your back, as well as an extra year or two of use.

Don't Be a Trail Fashionista: Dressing Your Infant

As we mentioned in chapter 2, it is very important to consider the weather and dress your baby appropriately. Remember, proper clothing is not a fashion statement on the trail—especially for babies—but rather an essential piece of equipment. Your 3-year-old son may look adorable in the light gray hoodie your hipster cousin from Brooklyn sent you last fall, but if he's not warm enough, he's going to be miserable and so are you.

For the most part, the clothes your baby wears at home will be fine. You don't need to buy him cute little hiking booties or adorable sandals unless you really want to. Besides, your parents have probably already sent him a pair anyway.

The sun often breaks through even the most covered canopy, so dress your child as though he will be in the sun for the duration of your hike. Another option, particularly if you live out west, is to carry an umbrella (if your carrier doesn't come with a sun canopy already). You could even attach it to your pack so that it's hands-free. Just be sure to check occasionally that it hasn't shifted away from your baby mid-hike.

If you live in a colder climate, pack warm gloves for those extremities. If you don't have warm gloves, a couple pairs of socks on each hand will do nicely; just make sure they stay on. Either tuck them in the sleeves of the child's jacket or tape them loosely so as not to restrict his circulation.

Your little one also needs warm socks (preferably wool, since they will keep him warm even when wet), shoes, and a big ol' hat in cold weather. Changing a dirty diaper in chilly temps requires exposing your child's skin. At a minimum this will be uncomfortable for him, and if it's particularly messy, the prolonged exposure could even be dangerous. Consider clothing that allows quick access for tackling diaper blowouts on a hike.

Remember to cover those extremities when you're hiking in cold weather.
MP (MEGAN PETERSON) PHOTOGRAPHY

In general, when you hit the trail with a young child, the items you typically carry in a diaper bag—Vaseline and other ointments, climate-appropriate outerwear, a change of clothes, extra diapers and wipes for those inevitable blowouts—instantly become "gear." Just be sure to bring plenty of plastic bags to carry out the . . . um . . . well, you know. Because in all our years of hiking, we've yet to come across one of those odor-killing diaper pails on the trail.

Papoose (Part Two): Finding the Right Kid Carrier

After 6 months of age, your child can face outward in the carrier. And if your baby is at all like ours, she's going to love having an unobstructed view of nature—and being the line leader. But depending on the support given by your baby carrier and the weight of your child, carrying babies 6 months of age and older can really start to hurt your lower back. When the back pain begins, you'll know it's time to shorten your outings, do some lower back exercises (three cheers for planking!), or consider switching to a backpack carrier before your child turns 1.

Deuter, Osprey, and Kelty are popular pack companies that make a variety of kid carriers. If you plan to hike with your infant by yourself, look for one with plenty of pockets for food, gear, and first-aid items. Ideally, at least some of these items will be accessible *without* having to take off the pack. If you usually hike with another adult or an older child, consider a lighter kid carrier with less storage capacity.

Another feature on some kid carriers is a built-in cover that provides shade for your precious cargo. As with the umbrella idea, this is particularly beneficial out west. Test the shade cover to make sure it's not leaving any areas exposed.

The most important consideration is *who* will be wearing the kid carrier. If you and a partner plan to share the child-carrying duties, try to find a pack that's comfortable for *both* of you. What works for a 6-foot-2, 200-pound man will probably be different from what works for a 5-foot-2, 120-pound woman. If the torso length and body weight between parents is drastically different, look for a pack with plenty of adjustable straps and buckles to accommodate both body types. And take good notes when the salesperson explains them to you because all those moving parts can get tricky.

When buying a new kid carrier, prioritize storage space, comfort for all, and accessible pockets.
BECKY EVANS

Feeding Time

Nursing on the trail is a piece of cake because you can stop whenever and wherever you want. If you're a nursing mother who's hiking for an extended period of time *without* your infant, though, be sure to pack a manual breast pump. Otherwise you'll carry a lot of extra weight (and discomfort) in your chest.

Mothers who use formula might need to think a little more creatively. You can always try to give your baby formula without heating it up. But your baby may not like it, and the cooler formula will require her to use extra energy to heat it up to her body temperature. To warm up formula, try boiling water for at least 1 minute to purify it (3 minutes if you're above 6,600 feet). Then use a thermometer to determine when it's cooled off to that ideal 98°F temperature. Remember, once the formula has been mixed it needs to be consumed or disposed of after an hour. Pack several extra bottles so that you can use a new one at each feeding to prevent bacteria from growing. If you bring a water purifier or boil a little extra water at each feeding, you can wash the bottle out with clean water and a little soap.

Quality Kicks: Shoe Selection

If you're hiking with an infant, toddler, or preschooler, we highly recommend investing in quality footwear for the kids. Learning how to toddle about is hard anywhere, let alone over roots and rocks. The last thing you want is for your little guy to slip and slide over muddy terrain or walk the last quarter-mile back to the car in agony because the soles of his shoes are too slick or the fit is a little too snug.

The same goes for parents too. Whether you're carrying your child on a 5-mile hike, helping your 1-year-old take his first steps on the trail, or trying to keep up with your prekindergartner as she makes her way up a creek bed, make sure you have durable, protective footwear *with a good tread*. Do everyone a favor, and don't add flip-flops to the equation.

Don't be afraid to let your kids explore—just be sure to keep a close eye on them.
MP (MEGAN PETERSON) PHOTOGRAPHY

ELEMENTARY SCHOOL

Elementary school–age kids are loads of fun to hike with—they're more on the move and can schlep some of their own gear. But they can also lack self-awareness, especially when it comes to how much they can do—versus *think* they can do. Here is some gear to consider when outfitting this age group.

Camel Up: Hydration Systems and Backpacks

A lot of the gear you use on the trail for elementary school kids will be the same things they use in school. For example, you can use the backpack he takes to class for extra clothes and trail food. Children shouldn't carry more than 25

Trail Mix

The last thing you want is for hiking to become complicated. Remember, at its core, hiking is simply walking in a natural setting. So most of the items we bring with us—including snacks—can and should be very simple. This Trail Mix section offers a trio of three-ingredient snacks that don't require any cooking.

Three-Ingredient Snacks

Pizza Crackers

1 8 oz. block of cheese

1 stick salami or pepperoni

1 sleeve of round crackers (rice or wheat)

Optional: small bag of sun-dried tomatoes or jar of pesto

Slice the cheese and salami. Then let your family assemble their mini pizzas however they like on the crackers. If you are feeling fancy, include sun-dried tomatoes or a small jar of pesto for an added flavor burst.

Bacon-Wrapped Dates

1 8 oz. package Gouda or other semisoft cheese

1 8 oz. package pitted dates

1 2.5 oz. package fully cooked bacon

Impress your friends and loved ones with this sweet and salty snack. First, cut the cheese into bite-size pieces. Next, stuff it into the already pitted dates. Finally, wrap a piece of precooked bacon around your Gouda-filled date. Voila! An hors d'oeuvre that's sure to please.

No-Cook S'mores Sandwich

1 13 oz. jar marshmallow creme

1 14 oz. box graham crackers

1 13 oz. jar chocolate hazelnut spread

©THINKSTOCK.COM/BHOFACK2

S'mores are quintessential trail food. But what if you don't want to bother with a fire, or if you hike in an area where fires aren't allowed? Not to worry! These delicious s'mores sandwiches fill the void without the chore of setting up and then extinguishing a fire. Just slather some marshmallow fluff on one graham cracker, a dollop of chocolate hazelnut spread on a second, mash them together, and enjoy. This treat promises to be just as sweet and sticky as the original campfire version.

percent of their body weight. (Incidentally, the same is true for adults.) So if you try to outfit your child with a full-size overnight pack complete with a hip belt and a plethora of storage space, you'll end up loading him down with too much weight. On the other hand, the relatively compact size of his school pack is a simple, easy way to limit how much he carries but gives him plenty of space for clothes, snacks, a water bottle, and maybe a sketch pad or journal so he can reflect on how his parents saved him from getting scoliosis as a child.

"Hiking at night is an adventure your family really should try."

If you decide to buy a hiking-specific pack, look for one with an internal hydration system. Many of the outdoor packs today come with a preinstalled water bladder and hose. The nice thing about this system is that the hose is usually affixed to one of the shoulder straps, so it's literally right there in front of your kid's eyes. Of course this may mean nothing to your 8-year-old; you'll still need to remind him to drink every so often.

A lot of school packs have a compartment for laptops—it's usually the one closest to the straps. This also happens to be where hydration systems usually rest in daypacks. If you're going with the old school backpack approach, buy a bladder and simply slide it in where the laptop usually fits.

Water bottles are another great way for your kids to carry fluids on the trail, but you need to remind them to drink more often if their bottles are stored inside their packs—as they say, out of sight, out of mind. If you buy a new water bottle or hydration system, choose one that's BPA-free. (Some research has shown that BPA may have possible health effects, especially for infants and young children.) BPA-free products can be found almost everywhere, and they're no more expensive than the alternative.

Hiking Poles

Starting around age 5, consider introducing your child to hiking poles—not only for long trips but for short day trips too. Hiking poles can be great tools on the trail. They offer a little *oomph*, allowing you to use your upper body on the uphills and taking stress off joints on the downhills. The downside is that they prove to be a terrific weapon against siblings. But then, doesn't everything? Just make sure your child has the coordination and maturity to handle a set of poles before adding them to your hiking routine.

An affordable alternative to hiking poles is a set of children's ski poles. You may already have some at home. Some kids prefer using two poles; others gravitate toward only one. Allow your children to try both methods and pick the one that feels right to them.

Star Light, Star Bright: Night Hiking

One of the most useful and fun pieces of gear you can give a young child is a strong flashlight or headlamp. Hiking at night is an adventure your family really should try because you can observe so many wonderful things in the dark that you might not notice during the day. Consider taking your child on a night hike to listen for hooting owls and other nocturnal goings-on. Or hike to a meadow where there's not much light pollution and scan the sky for shooting stars or constellations.

Brew trained for an ultramarathon years ago and went for a run in the dark since some portions of the race were at night. He'd never done a night run before but *completely* fell in love with it because it's a totally different experience. He ended up seeing a trail he'd been on dozens of times in a completely different light.

Prior to your night hike, just be sure to become very familiar with the trail, confirm you're not somewhere that's only open from sunup to sundown, and pack extra batteries or a backup light source.

Optional Gear for Your Budding Explorer

Here are two pieces of gear to consider for the hike that your elementary school kid will love: a magnifying glass and binoculars. A magnifying glass can provide hours of entertainment by transforming seemingly ordinary leaves, flowers, and insects into intricate masterpieces. One caveat, though: Some young children love to burn things with the intense light that's channeled through a magnifying glass. This can be a cool science experiment when done properly and with adult supervision, but it can also be very uncool when unsupervised children start fires or burn insects just for kicks. Make sure your child always uses the magnifying class appropriately.

Binoculars can help you spot wildlife or get a better view of a mountain range far off in the distance. They're also a useful piece of emergency equipment if you or someone in your group happens to get turned around. Binoculars come in all sizes and price points. Unless you're a birder or already geek out on binoculars, opt for pocket-size ones for space. And remember, all this extra equipment adds weight.

Hiking poles can be fun for little ones, but make sure they don't poke themselves—or their big sister.
STEPHEN PACK

real story

Tethered Together

Mariposa had always been an active child. She crawled with unbelievable speed and precision and began walking sooner than I could have anticipated. By the time she turned 5 I wondered just how soon before she could accompany me on backcountry adventures. While I had grand expectations for her abilities as a hiker (and hopefully someday a mountaineer), I certainly didn't want her earliest memories in the mountains to be filled with misery. That's why I was hesitant to commit to our first backpacking trip together as daddy and daughter.

By the summer of 2014, I decided it was time. When I told my friends I was planning on hiking with Mariposa to First Lake, a turquoise-blue cataract nestled high in the Sierra Nevada near the town where I grew up, I heard a litany of concerns. "What about the altitude?" "Beware of the sun exposure!" "Do you think she will really walk all that uphill?" Just as I began to question my intentions, a good friend who had introduced countless young people to the mountains offered this sage advice: "Better bring a tether."

I had never put my dog on a leash, let alone my child, and the thought of a tether seemed silly. Garland Rhodes, a lifelong Big Pine resident, must have seen the look of disbelief in my face, so he said, "Have you ever seen baby elephants walking with their parents? They hold on to a tail and can walk for hours. As long as children have something to hold on to, they can walk and walk and walk. And you don't want to try holding their hand up a steep, rocky trail."

So on the eve before our big trip, I received what was to be the absolute best advice for successfully hiking uphill with a wee one. I applied the wisdom of my good friend and attached a 3-foot length of tubular webbing to the bottom of my backpack, with an overhand knot tied at the end. I left it dangling for Mariposa to hold on to whenever she wanted it, and it worked like a charm. We were able to cover 5 miles of terrain in as many hours, with significant elevation gain. She walked steadily with the tether in one hand and a stuffed animal in the other.

*Mariposa at First Lake
in the Sierra Nevada*
MATTHEW J. NELSON

Along the way we saw a dozen hikers who could not believe that a 5-year-old was trekking into the High Sierra. After lots of rests and snacks, we arrived at the most picturesque campsite in the world. Mariposa slept soundly shortly after sunset as I watched the stars emerge and reflect off the magnificent mirror pool of First Lake. We did it. The sense of accomplishment is something we still talk about to this day. The tether comes with us on every backpacking trip now, and I know that someday it will be me who is holding on while she charges uphill.

—Matthew J. Nelson

If you decide to camp on the trail with young children, the right overnight gear can be difficult to find. Many age-specific sleeping bags last only a year or two before your child outgrows them, so think twice before purchasing that top-of-the-line down-filled mummy bag for your kindergartner. If you don't mind carrying the bulk or weight—and if it's warm enough—you can use the same cotton sleeping bag your kiddo takes to her friend's house for slumber parties. Another good option is sleeping *quilts*. These are typically made of down or synthetic down, so they're nice and warm. They can be wrapped around any size body just like a blanket and can accommodate children of varying heights and sizes. If you have an extra adult sleeping bag, fill the dead space at the bottom with extra clothes to keep your kid's feet warm.

MIDDLE SCHOOL

If your child is nearing middle school and is really digging the great outdoors (you'll know if he only rolls his eyes every *other* time you suggest a hike), it might be time to start investing in some trail-specific gear for him. However, finding gear that fits properly but lasts a long time can be very frustrating. Your seventh grader may still need kid-specific gear while his friends might already be shopping in the adult section of the outdoor store.

Don't Slack on a Pack

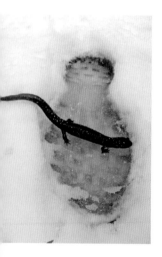

Having the correct-size boot or shoe is essential. Clearly this salamander didn't get the memo.
DAVIS FAMILY

Elementary school students can get away with less technical and supportive gear because they're usually going to carry less weight. But middle schoolers can start to carry more (don't let them tell you otherwise), so it's important for them to have proper fitting packs. Jen thru-hiked the Appalachian Trail the first time at 21 years old when she basically had the physique of a middle schooler. She started off with her brother's old external frame pack from his Boy Scout days, but having that cursed thing dig into her shoulders, rub her hipbones, and put undue stress on her lower vertebrae day after day was unbearable. That's when she realized it's just *not that much fun* to hike when every step hurts. There may be some growing pains breaking in a new pack, but eventually it should fit comfortably—as long as it's filled with the right cargo weight.

When it comes to finding a proper fit, take the one you want to buy on a test drive. Sure, it may feel great on your son when the cute sales girl is strapping it to his shoulders and asking him to promenade around the flat, straight aisles of the store like Derek Zoolander. But how will it feel when he's hiking up and down hills with a 20-pound payload on mile 9 of an 11-mile day?

Before you buy a new pack, ask the salesperson if you can take it out on a short day hike and return it if it doesn't fit properly. Most outdoor stores—even online retailers—have excellent customer service and generous return

policies. They should be agreeable to this arrangement so long as you return the pack in mint condition. Just be sure to try it out on a clear, sunny day, not when the meteorologist is forecasting a monsoon or a dust storm.

Consider something that your son or daughter can grow into but don't go overboard. A prepubescent 12-year-old boy should probably not carry a 5,000-cubic-inch pack that's better suited for a 60-year-old grandfather. It will be a decade before he grows into it, and by then he'll loathe hiking because he feels more like a pack mule than an adventurer. Get something reasonable.

Your child needs to know how to make adjustments to his pack so he can grow with it. Think of it as the pack equivalent of changing a tire. You shouldn't get one for him until he knows how to adjust it properly. It is amazing how many straps these packs have. All of them can be pushed and pulled to redistribute the weight; sometimes the difference between a perfect excursion and an excruciating one is as simple as tightening one strap or buckle.

What to Wear

When your child reaches puberty, clothing can make a big difference on a hike. For starters, he may be starting to sweat (and stink) more so he'll appreciate good wicking layers. And chafing also becomes an issue anywhere skin rubs together—under the arms, around the knees, and on the inner thighs—so it's a good idea to pack Vaseline, Body Glide, or another lubricant to help

Finding the right pack for your kids will make everyone's hike a lot more enjoyable.
SCOTT LIVINGSTON

Swimsuits are perfect attire for a summer hike beside a stream or lake.
ROBIN GIESELER

prevent friction. If you have a daughter, she may be wearing a bra by now. If she is, make sure she has a sports bra—something that wicks and has comfortable straps and seams—because it can be incredibly painful to have a bra strap rubbing under the weight of a pack on a long hike.

A good pair of wool or wool-blend socks is a crucial piece of gear if you're hiking in cold weather, snow, or rain. In fact, wool socks can be even more important than hiking boots. If sticking to relatively mild terrain—dirt, mud, and the occasional stream crossing—any sort of basketball, tennis, or cross-training shoe should work fine for most types of hiking, especially for greenways, nature preserves, and other urban settings. If the shoes have at least a little tread on them, they should be fine for more rugged trails too. Boots are wonderful, but they can be tougher to break in as well as expensive. They also might not be worth the investment until your child's feet stop growing.

HIGH SCHOOL

Ah, high school—a hormonal war zone. Sometime in this age range, children typically stop growing. That's when you can start collecting essential quality, long-lasting gear for your kids—backpack, sleeping bag, and footwear.

Unlike literature, there are typically no "young adult" sections in the outdoor store, so peruse the adult aisles to find the right fit. Consider starting small and adding a few items to your gear collection each year. This is an affordable way to collect the things your child needs while also making sure you don't spend pots of money on something he'll lose interest in a few years down the road. It can also be an effective carrot to dangle in front of him ("If you make honor roll next quarter . . .") or a fun way to prepare together for an extended outing.

Finding Their Niche

At this point, your children may be forming their own wilderness identity. If they are, woohoo! Your diabolical plan to get them interested in "nature 'n' stuff" has worked. Their interests naturally impact the gear they want; so if you haven't already, it's time to invest in some quality equipment for them.

"Shake Down" Before You Leave Town: What to Take and What to Leave Behind

A good exercise to perform with your teenager is to do a pack "shakedown" at home. A shakedown is the process of emptying out all the gear and equipment you plan to take on a hike and going through it all with a fine-tooth comb. This is a great way to talk to your kids about what you *need* on a hike versus what you *want*. You can cover required items listed on American Hiking Society's "10 Essentials of Hiking"

Trail Tech

Smartphones

Smartphones are a terrific piece of hiking equipment, and preinstalled apps can turn your phone into a digital multi-tool. For example, the flashlight on your iPhone probably isn't strong enough to use when you're actually walking, but it will work just fine if your headlamp goes out and you need to find a trail shelter or set up a tent after dark. Most smartphones also come with a compass feature that is accurate and easy to read. Just be sure to calibrate it before each use, usually by rocking your phone back and forth and side to side.

Since smartphones are one of the few pieces of equipment that can get ruined on the trail, invest in a good protective phone case, preferably one that's waterproof. (Ziplock bags also work well.) And consider portable chargers. They're as small as a tube of lipstick, provide extra charges for your phone, and are relatively inexpensive. Just remember, even with your cell phone and a backup charger, to always bring an old-fashioned compass, a map, and a headlamp with extra batteries.

CYNTHIA BOWERS

(covered earlier in this chapter), and you can discuss what "luxury" items they'd like to take, such as a sketchpad and colored pencils or a book.

Remind your kids that every extra item in their pack means extra weight on the trail. Encourage them to try out different items so they can find their own personal way to connect with the outdoors.

Cell phones, when used responsibly by your teen, have their place on the trail as well. But a word about earbuds: You would not believe the number of people we approach on the trail who don't know we're there until we're right next to them because they're rocking out to the Stones or Taylor Swift. We love music as much as the next person, but we also like to escape to the wilderness to get away from noise, Top 40 hits included. If allowing your teen to listen to his beats is a compromise you're willing to make, no problem. But please, for his safety and the safety of your group, encourage him to only put in *one earbud at a time* so that, at the very least, he can hear you in an emergency or know that someone is about to pass him.

next step

Some of the best backpacking gear can't be found in your neighborhood outdoor store. A number of hiking enthusiasts are now making and selling cutting-edge equipment out of their homes, and they've become very popular with trail lovers throughout the country. The advantage of buying a piece of gear from a cottage industry is that it is typically much lighter than what you'll find on the rack at an outdoor store. And since it's not mass produced, it's much easier to have your gear customized. Search online for "cottage industry hiking gear" to find everything from homemade tents and hammocks to sleeping bags and hiking skirts to long underwear and windproof mittens. Cottage industry prices are usually competitive with the brand names in most backpacking stores.

If you have time, know-how, and an old sewing machine, consider making your own gear.

- ☐ Making your own gear is easy and affordable.
- ☐ Search YouTube for thousands of beginner-friendly project how-tos, like how to make a lightweight stove with a used soda can.
- ☐ For an extensive list of homemade gear items and patterns, search backpacking.net.

chapter 4

What to Expect When You're Exploring

Knowing what you're getting into when you take your family for a hike is essential to actually enjoying the experience.

Jen has hiked more than 13,000 miles on six different continents, and I've hiked several thousand myself in the United States and North America. We've encountered just about everything you can imagine on our adventures—hiking over active volcanoes and glaciers, being chased by emus and dive-bombed by owls, pelted with marble-size hail and struck by lightning. So not much surprises us.

But when Charley came into the mix three years ago, all that "expertise" went out the window. Let me give you an example. When she was almost 2 years old, we combined some work with vacation and took a two-week trip to Alaska. Neither Jen nor I had ever been to Alaska, so we were super excited to visit it. On our first full day as we drove from Anchorage to Valdez through several hundred miles of mountains, lakes, and endless evergreen forest, Jen turned to me and said, "This is completely *redefining* my idea of wilderness." Pretty much the entire fortnight was more of the same.

We were most excited about a three-day stay in Denali National Park. I researched the campgrounds and the bus schedule. We had top-notch gear for the cold September nights, and we carefully packed the food we'd eat so we wouldn't have to leave the park. The one thing we didn't account for, though, was that Charley refused to stay in her sleeping bag despite nighttime low temperatures in the teens. Not only did she refuse to stay in her sleeping bag, but she also refused to wear the long underwear we put on her because she was used to sleeping in just a diaper. Clearly, this made for a long night in the tent. After our second night of fitful sleep, we packed up around 5 a.m., left the park, and made a beeline to the only coffee shop in town.

Grand Canyon National Park
©THINKSTOCK.COM/MRVELL

Hiking in pajamas? Hey, whatever works!
STEPHEN PACK

The point is this: Jen and I had to erase every expectation we had ("Oh yeah, we can make it to that waterfall in a couple of hours . . .") and start fresh with the understanding that hiking with Charley would be a whole new ball game ("Um, we've been on the trail for an hour and we've gone half a mile. Let's just have lunch by this creek and skip some rocks, shall we?"). Once we had a new paradigm, we enjoyed ourselves a whole lot more.

Now you may not have as many miles on the trail as we do, but you have a world of experience with your kids. And while those experiences give you an *idea* of what to expect on the trail, they'll be just that: an idea. Start this new adventure slowly, give yourself and your crew some grace, and remember that mistakes often make the best memories. I guarantee you, thirty years from now Jen, Charley, and I won't be talking about that fantastic night of sleep we had at the Best Western in Valdez. No, we'll think back to the time we visited Denali National Park and hardly slept a wink because Charley wouldn't stay in her sleeping bag. And how delicious that coffee tasted as we watched the morning sun light up the mountain.

—Brew Davis

KEEP IT REAL: SET REALISTIC GOALS

One of our favorite expressions in the hiking community is "HYOH," or "hike your own hike." What that means is there's no right or wrong way to do things on the trail. If you want to take 6 hours to complete a 2-mile outing, stopping every 50 feet to identify plants or snap photos, super. If you aim to crank out 30 miles a day and complete the 2,600-mile Pacific Crest Trail in three months, by all means have at it. The "best" hiker will always be the one who gets the most out of the experience. So the way to become "better" at hiking is to enjoy yourself more every time you go out.

"Hike your own hike."

When you start hiking as a family, there's no reason to set unobtainable goals for yourself. If you do, you won't enjoy the experience as much—and the last thing you want is for your kids to view your time on the trails as a death march rather than an opportunity to explore Mother Nature's backyard.

The biggest rule of thumb for planning your family outings is to do it with the least-skilled hiker—*usually* the youngest member of the group—in mind. Setting realistic goals and expectations from the beginning and increasing them gradually should help you avoid potential meltdowns from your kids— or your frustrated partner. As in life, everyone in your family will face unique obstacles and realities on the trail; your ability to anticipate and address them will provide your crew with the best possible experience.

PRESCHOOL AND YOUNGER

Hiking with a newborn can be intimidating. Because *everything* with a newborn can be intimidating. But hiking is—at least in our minds—one of the best and easiest activities you can do together. Most babies are soothed by the rhythmic motion of being carried down a trail. And riding on a parent's chest puts the baby in direct contact with a warm body and a beating heart, which is very comforting for a newborn. Car commercials show parents driving around the neighborhood to get their little one to fall back asleep, but taking Charley for a walk or hike worked just as well for us.

For new moms, hiking is a form of exercise that can help shed extra baby weight. And unlike most aerobics classes or gym workouts, it can be performed with baby in tow.

Starting early helps you gain strength gradually as your child continues to grow. You'll be more likely to go from carrying a 9-pound newborn on your chest to toting a 24-pound toddler on your back with little discomfort and a decreased risk of injury. If you and the baby hike with a spouse, partner, or friend, ask the other adult to carry the daypack with snacks, water, first-aid kit, and extra diapers. Even without a trail companion, you can still

strike out on your own by carrying a lightweight daypack in back and your kiddo up front.

When your child transitions to your back—this typically happens between 6 and 12 months of age—you may not feel as comfortable at first or be able to go as far with the heavier load. In fact, if you chart the average distance covered by parents with children from newborn to 5 years of age, you might be surprised that it's not a straight line where distance increases with age. Rather, it's an inverse bell curve. You'll probably hike *farther* with a newborn than you will with a heavier infant. You'll probably also go farther with an almost-1-year-old than with a toddler (you know, the one who refuses to ride in the kid pack but has not mastered walking in your living room, let alone on a rock-strewn trail). Only when your child becomes more comfortable walking on his own will your miles increase again. Around that same time, he'll turn into a "threenager" and will rip your graph to shreds, then torch it in your campfire.

Oscar the Grouch: Avoiding a Trail Meltdown

Charley and Brew throwing rocks in Minnesota while on a trail break
DAVIS FAMILY

As a parent you know that once toddlers or preschoolers have a meltdown, it is hard for them to recover in motion. Instead, it takes a reset—usually a nap—to restore harmony. So when you hit the trail with your young hiker, as with a road trip or other lengthy time commitment, try to get him squared away beforehand rather than anticipate his needs during the hike. Young children usually get cranky when they're hungry, tired, or thirsty. (Who are we kidding? *We* do the same thing.) And since a hike may take you and your kids out of your normal routine—including exerting more energy and burning more calories than usual—you should stop early and often for snack and water breaks. If you wait until your kids are hungry or thirsty, it's probably too late.

Regardless of the distance you cover, you may be surprised by how long your youngster will stay outdoors. In pleasant conditions, she may enjoy spending the better part of the day outside. As an infant, Charley always liked lying on a blanket and looking at the clouds. As a toddler she could throw rocks in lakes or ponds for hours

Trail Mix

When you hit the trail, offer your kids a snack that provides energy right away and also sticks with them for the duration of the hike. The best way to do that is with a healthy balance of proteins and carbohydrates, not to mention plenty of vitamins and minerals. If you're in a pinch, an energy bar will suffice. But if you have the time, why not make a quick and easy snack at home that's got plenty of carbs and protein without some of those less-desirable processed ingredients? This no-cook treat is called the Powerball, and when you eat it, you'll feel like you won the lottery.

The Powerball

3 cups powdered milk

2 cups natural peanut butter (smooth or crunchy)

1 cup raw honey

¾ cup wheat germ

½ cup granola

Optional coating: chocolate chips, sesame seeds, pecan pieces, or coconut flakes

Stir all ingredients and mix thoroughly. Next, roll the power-packed batter into 1-inch balls. Stick them in the fridge and—presto!—Powerballs!

Feel free to throw in some other sweet and salty morsels—chocolate (or carob) chips, sesame seeds, pecan pieces, coconut flakes, etc.

If you're hiking on a hot day or an overnight, stick your Powerballs in the freezer and allow them to thaw slowly as you walk. Remember: Honey is not recommended for children until they're 1-year-old. And these tasty nuggets do contain nuts, so be sure to keep them in the right hands.

(so could Brew). Now that she's 3, she enjoys searching for insects and salamanders in creeks for just as long. So don't be surprised if it's *you*, and not your newborn or preschooler, who decides it's time to wrap up the hike.

ELEMENTARY SCHOOL

Hiking with elementary school kids can be a surprising mix of bursts of seemingly endless energy and lulls where the child is on the brink of a meltdown. It's this inconsistent pacing that can make outings both refreshing and tiring for you as the parent. Here's what you can expect.

Snack time
PETER DARGATZ

Elementary school kids need help pacing themselves on the trail.
©THINKSTOCK.COM/
ERPRODUCTIONS LTD

Keeping Up with the Joneses: Maintaining a Steady Pace

Once your child reaches pre-K, you may find yourself getting more miles in on the trail. With most 5-year-olds, expect to cover a mile or mile and a half an hour over moderate terrain; just don't expect that pace to be *consistent*. Hiking with a second grader can often feel herky-jerky. Her youthful enthusiasm combined with her complete lack of awareness for a little thing called "pacing yourself" can lead to impressive bursts of energy followed by prolonged periods of distraction and stagnation. Just know that at some point you will likely struggle to keep up and then, a short while later, be begging her to take just a few more steps.

To avoid this erratic pace, consider challenging your youngster to stay within 20 or 30 yards of you as you move along the trail, which allows her to explore nature a bit while also keeping up. If that's not enough, this age group responds well to incentives. Consider breaking out a bag of fruit chews or pretzels and offering one every time you reach a trail marker or travel 100 yards. There's no shame in using the blinding power of food to motivate your children.

Children under age 5 have a wonderful attention span for being outdoors; elementary school–age hikers, not so much. And the fact that they *sort of* (but not really) understand distance and time can make it harder for them to conceptualize that there's a finish line. Telling your 7-year-old that it's just another quarter-mile to the waterfall doesn't mean much to her and can lead to some serious whining.

real story

Rewards on the Trail

My parents were hikers and mountain climbers, raising my siblings and me in the culture, so it seemed fitting to expose my six daughters to the great outdoors whenever possible. My second daughter, Lynn, at age 13, saw things differently. Hiking was *stupid*—although I don't recall that to be the exact term she used.

While on the Grassy Pond Trail in Baxter State Park in Maine, we crossed over a bog bridge. The 16-foot-long, 6-inch-wide bridge ran up a narrow brook, with one end of each section rising up when the opposite end was stepped on, creating a seesaw effect. Five of the girls were having fun; one was not. Each girl prepared to cross the mucky section, and that's when my idea hit. I'd use my stopwatch to see who can cross the bog bridge the fastest without falling in.

Five eager contenders lined up for their chance at the prize—an old, worn-out hiker patch with "The Fisher Cat Award" penned on top. Lynn stood back, pretending to be disgusted, while her sisters took their turns. One after the other they ran across—first Jana in record-breaking time, then Jill beating her out. Lisa fell in what we dubbed the alligator pit, and Angie did a windmill at midsection from laughing too hard. Finally, little Susan gave it her best shot for a seven-year-old. Then we turned to see Lynn standing at the starting line. Having forgotten she was "cool," she raced across to beat her sisters' times by seconds, winning the much-coveted patch. This game broke the ice and saved the day. We finished the hike into Grassy Pond and had a memorable day in a beautiful park.

—Lainie Winchell

Baby cairns
DAVIS FAMILY

But never fear. You have a few tricks up your sleeve. First of all, plan in advance for the anticipated meltdown. Bring along a toy or two—a coloring book, or a magnifying glass that gives the kids time to gather a second wind when they hit the wall. Beyond that, there is a host of activities that you can engage your children in, either during a break or while you're hiking; we'll talk about these more in chapter 6, Games and Activities. Check out the Appalachian Trail Conservancy's "hiking games and activities" page (appalachiantrail.org). There are dozens of other trail organizations and hiking clubs with similar lists. A lot of visitor centers at nature preserves and city, state, and national parks have junior ranger programs and activity sheets that your child can work on. And a lot of them reward kids with a patch or certificate of completion, which gives your child a sense of accomplishment and ownership over the experience.

Trail Tech

Noteledge

We all want our kids to connect with nature in meaningful ways, but it can be tedious carrying all the things that foster their unique interests (sketchbook and journal and SLR camera and GoPro and the list goes on). What's an empowering parent to do?

Enter Noteledge, an app that combines all these artistic ventures into one downloadable tool. It lets you scribble, sketch, journal, and upload videos and photos from your Apple device. Besides introducing your kids to various media, Noteledge is great for creating scrapbooks of your family adventures. Do the work yourself, let your kids take the reins, or—if everyone's not sick of one another after your day hike or overnight—work on the project together. Imagine e-mailing Grandma and Grandpa a nature sketch by your third grader with a journal entry from your seventh grader and a video of Dad tripping over a root and landing in a juniper bush? Noteledge is free to download, but if you find yourself making scrapbooks of all your hikes, consider investing in the premium version.

You Catch More Flies with Honey

Although it may be harder to encourage elementary school children to cover a substantial distance with any sort of fluidity, they still take a great deal of pride in their accomplishments. Compliment your reluctant hiker *before* she hits the wall ("Wow, you're really climbing up this hill like a champ!" or, "I didn't think you could go this far, but you've done an amazing job.") and you may find that she has an extra gear you didn't know about. You'll also give her something to build on so that next time she's willing to hike a little farther, climb higher, or tackle an even tougher trail.

On the other hand, the "suck it up" pep talk generally doesn't go over too well with this or any age group. More often than not, it leads to more whining and complaining, and perhaps even an impromptu trail sit-in. Since you're on a "family" hike, you need to follow the *family's* agenda—not your own—which

means you might be the one who has to suck it up this go-round. If you end up missing that "can't miss" view or that "perfect" swimming hole, just chock it up as a learning experience and make the proper adjustments for your next hike.

MIDDLE SCHOOL

As with many other family dynamics, hiking roles shift when your kids near middle school. Up until fifth or sixth grade, they've been inspiring you to view the trail with fresh eyes, restoring your childlike wonder. They've reveled in the ordinary, burned off excess energy, splashed in mud puddles, and caught fireflies.

When your kid hits middle school, though, a mud puddle becomes just a mud puddle again—something to be avoided rather than splashed in. You may have luck jogging your middle schooler's memory, but if you don't that's OK.

Take What the Trail Gives You

One of our favorite sayings when we're participating in trail races is "take what the trail gives you." That means go with the flow; don't push too hard on the uphills or hold back too much on the downhills. If there's a natural rest stop, take it. And if there's a long stretch without any, push on through.

The same can be said of your 11-year-old. He or she is becoming more social, spending more time texting with her friend down the street or hanging out at his buddy's house after school. So if you want your kid to dig the

"Take what the trail gives you."

outdoors, why not encourage him or her to invite a friend or two along? What better place for them to connect with one another than on the trail? Give them the appropriate amount of space so you don't disrupt their mojo. If you play your cards right, it could become a "thing" that your kids and their friends really enjoy. *Now* who's the cool one? You are. Way to go!

All in all, hiking with a preadolescent is mostly a mind game. By this time they are mini-adults and often have more energy than their parents. If they are in decent shape, they can cover big miles and stay outside for most of the day. Your primary development difficulties when hiking with them will not be physical but rather mental and emotional.

Preteens don't want to be *forced* to do anything, so it's more important than ever for you to include them in the process. Allow them to choose the destination and distance, select the trail food at home, or cultivate skills that are unique to them. Even if you are the driving force, make sure they have *some* control. By doing this, you encourage them to take ownership of the experience, and you may manage to sink those roots a little bit deeper into the trail.

HIGH SCHOOL

As your children transition to high school, they're going to have more on their plate. If you're lucky, they'll hit the books pretty hard, thinking about their GPA, their SAT score, the college admissions process, and how their transcript looks. Or maybe they'll be fully immersed in the social scene, thinking about what they're doing after the football game on Friday night or who's taking them to the winter dance. Regardless, high schoolers face pressures of all kinds—academic, social, extracurricular—and the trail can be the perfect antidote for all that chaos, allowing your teen to decompress mentally and physically.

Kids this age also go through all sorts of hormonal changes. Everyone develops at different rates, and it is easy for teens to feel like their bodies are always on exhibit. But the trail can be an oasis for them, a place that can improve their self-image. It can also be the perfect venue for important conversations, but you need to let those develop organically.

Play It Cool: How to (Not) Talk with Your Teen on the Trail

When we set out on our first long-distance hike together in Colorado, I felt as though I had to carry on a conversation every minute of the day. It wasn't until we'd hiked 50 miles or so through the San Juan Mountains that Jen whirled around and said, "You know, we don't have to talk *all* the time." This was a revelation. As it turns out, you don't need to make the hike interesting with small talk. Hiking is interesting enough without it.

*An afternoon
beach hike*
DAVIS FAMILY

The same is true of hiking with your teen. You don't have to fill all that space and time with a heavy, premeditated agenda. If you force the issue at the trailhead or turn every outing into a lecture on sex, drugs, or grades, your kid will clam up, finish the hike as quickly as possible, and reject every hiking overture you make for a while. But if you're willing to simply walk with your teenagers and let them drive the conversation, you might be surprised at how much they bring up and how much you can learn about your kids.

Give your teens some space with activities and camp chores. After all, they're growing up. If your son wants to filter the water, let him. If your daughter wants to carry the GPS and track your route, make sure she understands what she's doing and then let her run with it (though let's face it, she probably knows more about the technology than you do). The teens we've worked with love building, tending to, and putting out fires. As long as you go over basic fire-building principles and safety concerns, they should be able to handle it without incident.

One other note about hiking with your teenagers: Popular books like Richard Louv's *Last Child in the Woods* have done a terrific job of outlining the benefits of getting young people outdoors. If you live in a forward-thinking school district or send your children to an independent school, your kids may be able to use your family backpacking trips as an independent study. It would require some initiative—your teen may have to submit some forms and write a research paper or two—but wouldn't it be amazing for him or her to receive P.E. credits for your spring break hike on the Appalachian Trail or your week-long family vacation to Olympic National Park?

next step

Taking the entire family on an overnight can be a challenge, especially when trying to meet everyone's needs. But in some ways, spending the night in the backcountry can level the playing field and—gasp!—actually make things easier on you. Here's why you should consider this "next step" trip:

If you have time, know-how, and an old sewing machine, consider making your own gear.

- [ ] **Even out the group pace.** *You can load your older, faster child down with a bigger, heavier (but not too heavy) pack while giving your younger one a day-pack with the lightweight gear.*

- [ ] **Share the gear.** *When you backpack as a larger group, there's an economy of scales, meaning you and your group of four won't need four of everything, but rather one stove, one pot, one tent, one first-aid kit, etc.*

- [ ] **Delegate chores.** *Many hands make light work, right? At campsites, your oldest can set up tents while the youngest gathers kindling to start the fire. After dinner the youngest can filter water before bed and the oldest can hang the bear bag. Either way, you and your significant other can just prop your feet up beside the fire or soak in a hot spring while the kids do all the work. Or, if that makes you feel guilty, you can pitch in.*

- [ ] **Make kids happy.** *Kids are usually happiest when they can contribute and feel involved. Enlist their help with every part of the process. It may take more time on the front end to get organized and explain the tasks, but ultimately it will make the experience better for everyone.*

chapter 5

Honing Your Hiking Skills

One of my favorite things about hiking with other people, no matter their age, is that it gives you the opportunity to learn from their experiences, to share your own, and to discover something new together. Hiking with children is a great excuse to uncover all the things you wish you'd been taught growing up—or to relearn all those techniques for which you earned merit badges in Scouts.

While working with middle school students at a summer camp, I had to teach them the basics of orienteering. That's right, map and compass skills with an *actual* map and compass, not a GPS. I admit, my own skills were a bit rusty. But the good news was I had plenty of resources at my disposal that allowed me to brush up. With a little help from YouTube, some local guidebooks, and my peers at camp, I created a map-and-compass scavenger hunt. It was a huge hit, no one got lost, and afterward we all had a better grasp of reading maps and discerning direction.

If you relearn outdoor skills today, you may find that some of the approaches you were taught as a child no longer apply. Recently I prepared to take a group of teenagers on a trip through active bear country, so I practiced hanging a bear bag. Throwing a rope and hanging the bag with just *my* food was one thing, but the thought of hanging a bag with enough food for seven hungry 16-year-olds was a bit daunting. I discovered that using a carabiner and a simple knot allowed me to perform the task with ease, despite the added heft.

Leading high school groups on hiking trips regularly gives me the incentive to master a new technique or improve on an old one. And hiking with your children can do the same for you. My best teacher on the trail has been my daughter, Charley. She made me more aware of the weather conditions and of my on-trail surroundings. On my very first hike with her—an early-winter hike

Saguaros in Phoenix, Arizona
DAVIS FAMILY

several years ago—I vividly remember examining the clouds and gauging the wind so that I could make an informed decision about when we should head back to the car.

Charley has given us an enormous gift; she taught us to move slowly down the trail so that we take in every beautiful detail. When she started to put everything she picked up into her mouth, I explored edible plant identification to teach her which plants to avoid and which ones we can touch, smell, and even taste. We pick wild blueberries in late summer to make homemade muffins, but she usually eats more of them on the trail than she takes home. Last fall, my finicky eater even scarfed down a brothy soup I'd made from harvested cauliflower mushrooms.

Hiking with Charley has forced me to ask questions and to relearn important skills because when I'm on the trail with my family, the experience is never just about me. And I'm all the better for it.

—Jennifer Pharr Davis

HANDS-ON LEARNING

Even if you know very little about hiking or the natural world, you can still be an outdoor educator when you hike with your family and provide them with plenty of teachable moments. You can pursue whatever interests you, starting with simple observations and skills, or you can let your kids' questions determine what you research.

In any new environment, there's *so much* to learn. And this is especially true in nature. Pardon the pun, but learning on the trail happens organically. Encourage your kids to be inquisitive, and teach them how to find the answers, either on their own or with your help. A simple on-trail question ("How'd that tree get to be so big?") can turn into a wonderful science experiment at home (putting an acorn from the trail in water until it sprouts or even planting it in your yard).

Recent studies have shown children grasp and maintain information much more in a hands-on setting than when they're sitting at a desk surrounded by four walls. What better setting than nature for teaching children to be hungry, inquisitive learners? It's no wonder schools across the country have begun implementing outdoor units into their academic models.

The most important lesson to teach your family is how to move along the trail safely. On each hike, build on that foundation by adding a plant name here or a birdcall there. None other than Henry David Thoreau said, "It were as well to be educated in the shadow of a mountain as in more classic shade. Some will remember, no doubt, not only that they went to college, but that they went to the mountain." It's a wonderful thing to be a student of the trail.

Trail Tech

Flora and Fauna Identification Apps

Carrying multiple field guides in your daypack to bulk up on your knowledge of flora and fauna can be cumbersome. But several free or low-cost apps can help you identify your discoveries along the trail right at your fingertips.

If you are a birder, try the free Audubon Bird Guide or the Merlin Bird ID app. Both tools offer not just descriptions and photos but also recorded calls. iBird is another popular birding app. The pro version isn't free, but it uses the GPS and data on your phone to customize a list of potential sightings for you; it also records when and where you spotted different species.

For wildflower lovers, consider the Audubon Wildflowers app. With an index of nearly 2,000 North American species, you're likely to find information on whatever flower you discover. Try searching for wildflower apps specific to your region. For example, there is a great one for the Great Smoky Mountains called GSM Wildflowers. It only includes 200 species but is less overwhelming and easier to use than an index for the entire country.

PRESCHOOL

Infants, toddlers, and preschoolers are like sponges. No matter where they go or what they're doing, they're absorbing new sights, sounds, and smells. One great thing about being on-trail with a baby is that organic matter is completely different from what he or she experiences at home or in day care. A songbird sounds nothing like a talking doll, and the cool, imperfect feel of a rock is totally different from a smooth, plastic toy—everything is new and stimulating.

When we began hiking with Charley, we were entertained by how she liked to grab leaves or run her fingers over the bark of a tree. Still today, when she rides on our shoulders, she asks if we can meander this or that way so she can grab a branch that's caught her eye. Of course we have to remind her just to *touch* the branch rather than snap it off and use it on one of us like a jockey on a horse. But the point is that she was soaking up sights, sounds, and smells in the best possible environment and at the most impressionable age. And what could be better for your kid than that?

When your child gets older, use objects found on the trail to teach her about shapes, colors, and numbers. Play counting games with twigs, or pick out different-shaped stones from a creek and ask her to point out the oval. If you come across a patch of wildflowers, ask her to identify all the colors.

Kids increase their vocabulary at a remarkable rate, and the more words they're exposed to at an early age, the better prepared their minds are for kindergarten. So why not use the trail to expand their vocabulary? Around the same time that we started teaching Charley basic words like "bath" and "soap," we also taught her simple trail words like "creek" and "dirt." And, yes, that's because she always came home from our hikes filthy.

"Why not use the trail to expand [your kids'] vocabulary?"

Look, this isn't rocket science. You don't have to be a tree expert to teach your child words like "bark, "roots," "limb," "pine needle," or "evergreen." Just recognize all the teachable moments that present themselves on the trail. There is no better time to develop your child's wilderness IQ than before the age of 5. And by exposing her to the trails at such a young age, you establish a foundation for spending time in the outdoors that will stay with her for the rest of her life.

Charley looking at trillium in Vermont
DAVIS FAMILY

ELEMENTARY SCHOOL

As your children near kindergarten, their brains are still sponges. But because they have greater cognition and communication skills, you can see them grasp what they're learning more quickly and really run with it. Around this time, most kids start to spend much of the day inside, so it's all the more important to give them an avenue for physical, mental, and emotional exercise that's completely different from what they get when they're sitting in a classroom.

Poison Ivy, Poison Oak, and Poison Sumac

Since these kids are not underfoot when they're on the trail with you, and since they've got their colors and shapes down pat, you first want to cover how to identify—and avoid—poison ivy, poison oak, and poison sumac. These plants show up even on urban hikes along city pathways. Poison ivy and poison oak both have three leaves. You can teach your child the catchy saying "Leaves of three, let them be," but we always like to point out that half of all the ground cover in the forest seems to have three leaves. So either you avoid everything—which leaves you walking around like Indiana Jones in the *Temple of Doom*—or you learn a few other features of poison ivy. Here's what to watch out for:

Poison Ivy

- Shiny, pointed leaves
- Reddish in spring
- Yellow or orange in the fall
- Furry vine in winter

Poison Oak

- Clusters of leaves
- Some with fuzzy berries under the leaves (but you may be standing in a patch of poison oak if you can see them)

Poison Sumac

- Looks more like a shrub, with each stem sporting seven to thirteen opposing leaves (meaning they're directly across from each other and not staggered)
- Has green berries

The Touchables

The vast majority of plants can and should be touched, smelled, and even tasted. For example, mullein and lamb's ears are as soft as any furry friend you may have in your living room. Plants like wintergreen and sassafras are not only fun to smell but also to taste. To appreciate the beauty and fragrance of a wildflower with your kids, you don't have to be an expert, just an observant hiker.

Speaking of touchables, it's a good idea to give your young children a healthy respect for all wildlife, even the small, harmless ones. Since your child's gross motor skills aren't completely fine-tuned yet, you may want to be the one to pick up a ladybug or corral a salamander. You won't want him approaching snakes, no matter the size, and although it may be tempting to catch a butterfly, doing so can actually hurt its wings. Also, make sure your first grader knows that that black-and-white "kitty" is actually a skunk.

Several other plants make the "do not touch" list: cactus, briars and thorn bushes, and holly leaves. You can identify them easily by their prickly appearance.

Generally speaking, if you can keep everyone on the trail and in the clearing of a camp-ground, you shouldn't have to worry too much about these plants. Just don't go bush-whacking through unknown underbrush, and be careful when you gather firewood or make an impromptu pit stop. If you have a dog on the trail, keep it away from suspicious looking plants and be sure to give him a good scrubbing when you get home. Though these irritating oils can't be spread from person to person, they can stay on clothing for months or even years, so throw clothes in the wash when you get home, and remember that these plants are a hazard year-round.

Basic Hiking Skills

Speaking of identifying things, this is a good time to teach your child some basic hiking skills, such as **identifying cardinal directions.** When hiking at sunrise or sunset, point out that the sun always says "good morning" from the east and "good night" from the west. Or break out the old compass and teach the kids how to use it properly, which will reinforce cardinal directions while also providing an important trail skill.

Teach your kids how to **judge the time of day based on the sun's position.** (Here's a reminder: If the sun is far to the east, it's early morning. When it's overhead, it's midday or early afternoon; when it's to the west, it is late afternoon or early evening.) The sun can also be used to discuss winter and summer solstices (the shortest and longest days of the year) and the vernal and autumnal equinoxes (which kick off spring and fall, respectively). Observing the Earth and it's relation to the sun can explain why the north slope of a mountain has more snow and ice in winter or different vegetation in summer.

Basic camp chores are good for this group to learn, as they tend to be eager beavers. Setting up a tent is much easier with a helper—even a young helper—than without one. The helper can hold the poles in place while you maneuver the tent canopy. Have your kiddo help with packing up too, which makes the chore easier and faster; one person holds the stuff sack for a tent or sleeping bag, while another mashes it into its confoundedly small bag.

Teach your kids basic hiking skills early to lay a good foundation for later.
STEPHEN PACK

Know Your Clouds

Did you know you can interpret weather patterns from watching the clouds? Here are four basic cloud types to know:

Cirrus clouds are light, wispy, and high in the sky. They're often called "mare's tail" because they look like the tail of a horse. They usually indicate good hiking weather, but they can also indicate that a change is coming in the next 24 hours.

Stratus clouds sit very low and look a lot like fog. They're a uniform gray color and cover all or most of the sky. Light rain or mist can fall from stratus clouds, but the good news is you're unlikely to get soaked by a downpour.

Cumulus clouds look like big white (sometimes gray) cotton balls floating in the sky. They can indicate fair weather, but if they start to build up and take the shape of cauliflower, you'll want to head down the mountain—they are turning into thunderclouds.

Cumulonimbus clouds are large, dark clouds that reach high into the sky. They are thunderclouds, sometimes called "thunderheads" because they can be shaped like the head of an anvil. These clouds are indicators of rain, snow, lightning, hail, or even tornadoes. If you see them forming before your hike, you may want to take a rain check. If you are already out, turn back to the trailhead or find a safe place to take refuge.

Bryce Canyon National Park on a chilly fall afternoon
DAVIS FAMILY

Here's an important safety skill for a child to learn, and it starts with providing him with a **safety whistle** in case of emergency. We know, we know. This is a Pandora's box. But if you explain that *all* whistle blows mean something and warrant attention, he should grasp the importance of *using* and not *abusing* this new piece of equipment. There are three distinct calls that can be useful in a wilderness setting.

One blast of the whistle means "Where are you?"

Two blasts mean "Come back!"

Three blasts mean "Help!" This is the one most often used in emergency situations and is effectively an SOS call.

We should also repeat here what one wilderness survival website had to say: "There are whistles, and then there are *whistles*." The pink princess or Dora the Explorer whistle your daughter got for Halloween last year is not going to measure up in the woods, so go ahead and invest in a more durable, heavy-duty version. They're usually big, bright orange, and on a clear night they can be heard from a mile away. They also have terrific names like the Howler, the JetScream, and the Fox 40 Sonic Blast.

Another safety skill to know in an emergency situation is **how to use a safety mirror.** These typically come attached to compasses and are used to signal search-and-rescue aircraft. Because they can concentrate sunlight into a powerful, narrow beam, they can also be used like a laser pointer to annoy an older sister or drive the family dog crazy. Like safety whistles, they shouldn't be misused; the intensity of the beam can burn skin, leaves, insects, or whatever else it's directed toward.

MIDDLE SCHOOL

With all the changes kids face as they enter middle school—increased academic and social pressure, along with all the emotional and physical effects of puberty—it's not uncommon for them to sometimes feel lost. So this might just be the perfect time to teach them some navigational skills.

Intermediate Hiking Skills

Teach your child to read maps. With any map, discuss your route before you set out. And with a topographic map (a map with lines to indicate elevation), you can not only identify your route but also point out spots where the trail climbs and descends. If your child doesn't already know how, go over how to use a compass. Here's an easy way for the kids to learn: "Put red Fred in the shed." This means as long as red Fred (the magnetic north arrow) stays in his shed (the orienting arrow), you should be able to move confidently in the direction you want to go.

Middle school is the perfect time to teach your kids some navigational skills.
CHRIS RACHOR

With a topographic map, you can also point out bodies of water and bring up the idea of watersheds. If you're near a creek, play "Poohsticks," one of Winnie the Pooh's favorite games, to discuss concepts like upstream, downstream, eddy, and current. This simple pastime is played when people drop a stick or leaf in water on one side of a bridge (or log bridge) and wait to see which one comes out first on the other side. It's a fantastic way to **teach kids about where water goes.**

If you want to entertain a middle schooler for hours, give him flint and steel and **teach him how to start a fire.** With those fire-starting techniques, you also need to delve into fire safety, which is particularly important during late summer and in regions out west that are prone to wildfires.

There are several techniques for building a successful fire, but almost all of them start with a pile of dry kindling surrounded by a "tepee" or "log cabin" of small sticks. Make sure the fire can breathe and isn't smothered by large pieces of wood in the beginning. Flint and steel, matches, or a lighter can be used to start a fire. If you want a little help, cotton balls dipped in Vaseline, lint from your dryer, or even a handful of oily corn or potato chips can get your fire going on the trail. Use your body to screen the fire from wind, or position your tent to do this.

If you want to *completely* exhaust your preteen, encourage her to start a fire using a bow drill or bare-handed technique. Most middle schoolers don't have the strength or patience to make a fire this way, but she'll burn up lots of time and energy trying. And it may be a fun long-term goal for all of you. For more information on fire building and fire safety, check out smokeybear.com. You can keep the kids busy at home by having them track down how-to videos on the internet. And remember, as Smokey says, "Only you can prevent forest fires."

Knot tying is another fun activity for middle schoolers and is especially useful for fishing or hanging a bear bag. You can find plenty of information online about how to make and use different knots. Or you may want to purchase an inexpensive knot kit that comes with instructions.

Programming Note

Fire safety is dreadfully important; people's lives and livelihoods depend on your acting responsibly. As a general rule, neither parents nor children should start a campfire if there is an above-average risk of wildfires. If campfires are permitted, you still need to monitor them constantly while they burn. And the flames and embers need to be completely snuffed out before you turn your attention from the fire or pack up to leave the area.

Just because you don't see glowing embers doesn't mean the fire is out. Move the top layer of ashes around with a stick to see if any coals are still burning underneath. Then douse the fire with lots of water and spread the ashes around the fire ring until the coals are cool, dark, and wet. Do not build a fire or create a fire ring in a place where one does not already exist.

As a parent, you naturally want to point your children toward *safe* activities on the trail. But your kids are growing up, so it's also important to expose them to *calculated* risks to show that you trust them and that you think they're ready to assume more responsibility.

Carving and whittling with a pocketknife is one craft that can help build their skills. Start with a small, foldable knife to reduce the potential for injury, and to keep your middle schooler's pack weight down. Beyond that, **knife skills** are beneficial on the trail, in the kitchen, and as a general life skill. And learning to respect useful yet potentially dangerous objects is part of the maturation process. Besides, sitting beside your daughter as she learns to whittle is good practice for riding white-knuckled in the passenger seat when she's learning to drive in a few years.

Trail Mix

Recently we led a group of high school students on a four-day outing near Asheville, North Carolina. Just before dinner on the first night, one of the boys broke out a ziplock bag of beef jerky, passed it around, and mentioned that he'd made it himself. Judging by the group's reaction, you would have thought the kid had climbed Everest solo without oxygen.

You too can impress your family and friends by dehydrating savory strips of meat at home. And you don't even need a food dehydrator. All you need for this lightweight, high-protein, long–shelf life snack is an oven and a little patience.

Homemade Beef Jerky

3 pounds flank steak

12 ounces steak marinade (use your favorite store-bought variety or make your own)

Dash of pepper (or to taste)

(Optional) Crushed chili pepper

Cut the flank steak into consistent strips 4 to 6 inches long and ¼ inch thick. It's easier to cut even slices if you freeze the steak an hour before slicing it and use a long, sharp cutting knife. Put the strips into a sealable plastic bag or storage container, and coat them with your favorite marinade. Marinate the steak in the refrigerator for at least 3 hours. Remove it from the fridge and let it come to room temperature—about 1 hour.

Prepare the oven by covering the bottom with aluminum foil and greasing the racks with a nonstick spray. Preheat the oven to 175°F.

Drain the marinade off the steak and place the strips ½ inch apart on the baking racks. Add as much or as little pepper as you like; if you want to spice it up even more, sprinkle on some crushed chili pepper. Cook the jerky until it's completely dry, usually about 3 hours. Jerky stored in an airtight container can stay good up to three months.

HIGH SCHOOL

By the time your children are teenagers, they should be able to master—or at least grasp—any hiking skill you throw at them. Their more-mature bodies allow them to traverse rock scrambles, river fords, and snowfields that can prove too technical for younger children. They also can carry more weight and go farther now than just a few years ago, which opens the door for longer overnight trips in more remote settings.

Advanced Hiking Skills

Crossing rivers and snowfields. If you want to cross a river with your teen, study the area first. Check downstream for potential hazards (rapids, a logjam, etc.), and use a stick or hiking pole to test the current. If it's really strong and the water is more than knee high, you shouldn't attempt a ford. *Never* cross a creek or river above a waterfall, and never *ever* ford if you or your child doesn't know how to swim. Be mindful of flash floods in the area if there's been a lot of recent rainfall.

The wider parts of the river are usually shallower. Look for spots where the river is broken up into channels by sandbars. It's tempting to take your shoes off to keep them dry, but it's always advised to wear foot protection during a ford, which can prevent you from stepping on broken glass or a fishhook left

Zsofia (right), at 16, on her first winter hike (to Lonesome Lake Hut, Franconia Notch State Park, New Hampshire)
SARA HART

by an angler. Keep your feet drier by taking off your socks and removing your insoles before you cross.

When you are ready to cross, first unclasp your pack so that it doesn't weigh you down if you happen to fall in. Then slowly work your way toward the opposite bank, facing the current slightly upstream. Keep your head up; staring down at moving water can make you dizzy. Plant one foot firmly on the riverbed before lifting your other foot. If you have hiking poles, use them for stability, but be sure to plant them carefully and securely. When you get to the opposite bank, take a snack break to allow your shoes to dry out a bit—and to gaze at the river with a sense of accomplishment.

Use as much caution crossing a snowfield as you use fording a river. Don't expect to only find them when hiking in winter or spring; the Rockies, Sierras, North Cascades, and even the White Mountains of New Hampshire can have snowfields at the higher elevations late into summer, especially on the northern slopes. The ideal time of day to cross a snowfield is mid- to late morning. Too early in the day and the snow might still be frozen and slick; any later, the snow will be mushy and you could end up post-holing (plunging several feet through the snow)—or worse. Beware of any glacial runoff or snowmelt that could erode your route from underneath. Look for places where other hikers have success-fully crossed. And don't walk directly above steep pitches, if possible.

Adults should go first and create footsteps for teens to follow. Kick into the snow or stomp down several times to make a solid foothold before transferring your weight. A hiking pole can be a great tool for maintaining balance and for keeping your footing. If you think you'll do a lot of technical crossings, invest in some crampons for your feet and an ice ax for self-arrest (stopping yourself from a fall). The best way to self-arrest if you find yourself slipping down a snowfield *without* crampons or an ax is to get on your stomach, stick your bum out, and dig in as hard as you can with your elbows and toes. You can also use your hiking poles, or even a water bottle to slow yourself down. Slip-sliding down a slope isn't always a bad thing; glissading (a controlled slide on your feet or your bum) can be a fun way to get to the bottom of a snowfield quickly, provided there are no rocks in your path and that you feel comfortable doing it.

Hiking through the desert can be another fun adventure to tackle with your teenager. The desert often gets a bad reputation due to its heat and lack of water, but if you've ever read Wallace Stegner or Edward Abbey, seen the Grand Canyon, or walked through the slot canyons of southern Utah, you know how stark and stunning this landscape can be. Just be sure to remember your sunscreen, breathable clothing, and gallon jugs of water. And pay particular attention to the weather forecast, since the arid desert ground makes these areas especially prone to flash floods after a hard rain.

When hiking trickier, more advanced trails with your family, a very important skill to introduce is **mastering the functions of GPS (global positional system).** Younger children can also master the functions of a GPS unit, but you should cover traditional map and compass navigation with them before using GPS as an additional tool. Your teen will probably take to a GPS like a duck to water and will quickly be showing you new features you didn't know existed, like mapping your route, tracking elevation gain and loss, or providing a trip report that tracks your distance.

next step

You don't have to live off the land or be a "prepper" to benefit from a survival skills class. Learning primitive methods for starting a fire, constructing a shelter, and creating fishhooks or animal traps is useful and fun. Here are some ways to beef up your survival skills knowledge:

- ☐ *Take a survival skills class. Topics include building shelter, starting fires, and finding food and water.*
- ☐ *Look into all-day or all-weekend turbo courses offered by local survival experts.*
- ☐ *If time permits, consider courses that are a month- or semester-long.*
- ☐ *For self-instruction, read books about primitive skills and survival by experts like Tom Brown Jr.*

Tall pines, fishing lines, and a trail that leads to heaven
DAVIS FAMILY

chapter 6

Games and Activities

A lot of families have holiday traditions. There's backyard barbe-
cue and fireworks on the Fourth of July, turkey and football for
Thanksgiving, presents for Christmas or Hanukkah, and cheesy
cards for Valentine's Day. One of our holiday traditions is taking
hikes together, especially after eating too much pumpkin pie or corn bread
dressing. When we hit the trail with grandparents, nieces and nephews of all
different ages, grown-up siblings and in-laws, everyone has a different idea of
what hiking entails.

There's a classic *Saturday Night Live* skit where a family is fighting like
cats and dogs at the Thanksgiving dinner table until a 12-year-old girl walks
over to a stereo and turns on "Hello" by Adele. Everybody instantly for-
gets their troubles and starts singing along rapturously. Well, the trail is our
extended family's version of Adele.

There's potential for unending family drama surrounding the holidays,
and yet somehow we find harmony together on a hike. When you're walking
with a large, multigenerational group, it's really easy to observe individuals
connecting with nature in different ways. Charley and her 5-year-old cousin
like to pretend they are princesses on a forest adventure. To complete the
picture, they typically dress up in their *Cinderella* or *Frozen* costumes before
we go out. Even though they get their clothes dirty, their ensembles, combined with the environment, create some adorable photographs and lasting
memories.

The older boys, ages 5 to 55, love to hide behind trees and jump out to
scare everyone. They also love to skip rocks or aim at arbitrary targets whenever they have the chance. It always amazes me how a pebble-strewn beach
can provide hours of entertainment. Even when they get tired of tossing the

A little adventure on the trail makes for a more fun day.
DAVIS FAMILY

rocks, they start stacking them into creative-looking cairns. How they keep them balanced, I can never figure out.

A pair of binoculars usually gets passed around among the oldest and youngest hikers to identify different varieties of birds and distant animals. I'm not always convinced that my dad has actually spotting something. More likely he's just looking for an excuse to catch a breather. And some of my cousins use their smartphones to look for geocaches along the route.

Observing our family outing is a strong reminder that different people at different ages connect to the trail in different ways. It also makes me appreciate how activities can engage opposite extremes while still giving everyone an appreciation for the outdoors. I freely admit that one of the most difficult parts of going on a group hike is finding a game or project that everyone enjoys. The most popular one? Campfires and s'mores. There's just something about s'mores—they're odd and messy yet so sublime. Kind of like a family.

—*Jennifer Pharr Davis*

MAKE THE TRAIL FUN

Incorporating games and activities into your hiking adventure is a way of taking something fun and making it even more enjoyable. Games help you get through a tricky or long section without actually thinking about placing one foot in front of the other. Games also help you learn about your environment and connect with nature and your family in new and different ways.

The important thing is to balance structured activities with free play- and downtime. All of us, even children, have plenty of structure in our everyday lives, and a hike that is structured down to the minute with an agenda full of activities can feel like a commitment rather than an adventure. Being in nature with your family should allow you to feel free—free from demanding schedules and free to play silly games or do nothing at all but walk, depending on your mood.

Let your kids take the lead in introducing activities on the trail. They tend to know much better than we do how and when to play.

PRESCHOOL

Learning by play is a huge part of any preschool curriculum, and it's the same when you're out on the trail with your youngest hikers. Kids this age are experiencing nature for the first time—whether it's a wooded path in a state park in the countryside or a boardwalk through a marshland with the cityscape in the background. Chances are you won't hike very far with toddlers at first, but making the outdoors exciting and engaging from the very first outing will ensure that they'll associate fun with being in nature.

Charley playing in a stream in a sundress
DAVIS FAMILY

The Classics

Many of the games you play with your toddler at home translate perfectly to the outdoors if you just "trail them up" a bit.

Follow the Leader is a great game to play while you're out on a hike. A parent can take a turn being the line leader and encourage the rest of the family to march down the trail, pick up a stick and throw it (gently!), fly along like an airplane, walk backwards (carefully!), or pump their arms in circles and pretend to be a choo-choo train. Next, let your young child take a turn in the front of the line and see what moves he or she comes up with. This is a great game to play when you need to make some progress down the trail.

Simon Says can be incorporated into a hike. Use prompts like, "Simon says, 'Run to the next big rock.'" "Simon says, 'Find a wildflower.'" You get the idea.

Princess dresses and frilly tutus make trail exploration that much more fun.
KATIE CARDOSO

I Spy is a great way to teach young children how to identify colors, shapes, plants, and animals. You could say, "I spy with my little eye something that is round," "something red," "something with petals," "something living off something else" (a mushroom, for example). You might see if they can point out poison ivy—without touching it—a bee with pollen, or an ant carrying something much larger than itself. Regardless of what you *intend* for your child to "spy," you'll almost certainly be entertained by what he or she discovers along the way.

Most babies, toddlers, and preschoolers are fascinated with animals; incorporate them into your hike without actually having a too-close encounter by mimicking the animal noises and behaviors and letting your kids guess the animal. Lumber down the trail on all fours like a bear, dart down the path like a rabbit, flap your arms and hoot like an owl, or twist and hiss like a snake. Let your children imitate animals too, and don't be afraid to pick outlandish, nonnative species, like a peacock or koala. The more bizarre you get with the game, the more fun your kids will have.

Use your imagination when you're out hiking with young children; make up a story to share or act out along the way. The trail is a great place to re-create your kids' favorite fairy tale, book, or movie. If you haven't noticed, you may soon realize that almost every Disney plot has an extended outdoor scene. We mentioned earlier that we let Charley and her cousin don princess dresses on our hikes. Consider doing the same or even letting them do a little "method acting" and get into character before you leave the house—if you can stand it.

Sensory Games

Even babies can play games on the trail. Infants respond well when you appeal to their senses. If you hear a constant noise like a waterfall, a strong wind, or a field of crickets, cover your baby's ears then remove your hands to reveal the difference between the silence and nature's soundtrack. Think of it almost like playing peekaboo, but with their ears. Imitate the call of a bird, squirrel, or chipmunk, and see if your infant can follow along. Some of our most transcendent trail moments were those first few months when Charley had her initial encounter with something and just couldn't get over it, either expressing complete wonder or laughing her head off for minutes on end.

One of Charley's favorite games—and Brew's—is to write or paint with water on rocks. You can bring a paintbrush from home or just use your finger. All you really need is a body of water and some decent-size rocks. Let your son practice his ABCs, drawing shapes, creating a family portrait—whatever. The slate will be clean again in a minute or two, and he can start all over.

ELEMENTARY SCHOOL

Elementary school kids love the idea of organized play on and off the trail (Field Day, anyone?), so you do not have to work very hard to get this age group excited about games. Lucky for you, there's an almost endless supply that you can incorporate into your family's hiking experience. Some help your kids learn about their surroundings, some reinforce what they learn in school, and some are just oodles of fun for you and for them.

Ranger badges are a fun incentive for kids when visiting national parks.
TOM DAVIS

Educational Games

A really fun way to teach your kindergartner or first grader his ABC's is to play a letter search game. Ask him to see which letters he can find in the natural shapes of the forest. Maybe the acorn at his foot looks like an "O." There could be a rock formation in the shape of a "W" or a series of branches in the tree above his head that looks like an uppercase "A." See if he can find all twenty-six letters. You can even take photos of each and frame them for a fun, outdoorsy wall hanging in his bedroom.

Finding letters in nature can be pretty easy. Finding words? Not so much. But, you can *spell* words by snapping twigs or breaking limbs (ones already found on the ground, of course) and laying them out as letters on the ground. Brew used to write love notes ("LUV U") and encouraging messages ("U GO GRL") when he was supporting me on my Appalachian Trail hikes. Now he writes snarky comments on our trail runs like "U R 2 Slow." Ah, the joys of marriage.

Get to Know Your State is a fun activity that helps kids learn about their states. It's pretty straightforward and makes for a great school project (if your child has any say in the matter). The goal is to identify designated and well-known state symbols, like the flower, bird, animal, and tree. But you can really have fun with it (at the expense of your second grader) and compel her to track down lesser-known state symbols, like the insect, mushroom, seashell (if you're on the coast), even the fruit and nut. Challenge your child to re-create the state flag out of items found on a hike, or encourage her to write her own state poem or song.

Trail Tech

Disney

When you think of Disney you think of princesses, magic, musicals, and notorious villains. But Disney has also done quite a bit to expose children to the wonders of nature. Disney has put out some terrific wildlife documentaries that are perfect for cuddling up at home on a cold winter day or during a rainstorm. Bears, African Cats, Chimpanzee, Monkey Kingdom, Oceans, and Earth all do an incredible job of capturing animals up close and in their native habitat. Plus, Disney manages to write compelling, poignant narratives that engage your child throughout the entire film.

Disney's kid-friendly Disneynature Explorer is a free app appropriate for 4- to 8-year-olds. It features facts and games about a bear, lion, butterfly, chimpanzee, and sea turtle that encourage children to explore nature and view it through the eyes of the chosen animal. The award-winning app is captivating, thoughtful, and easy to use. And if your kids are more familiar with the Disney Channel than the great outdoors, this might be the perfect tool for getting them excited about nature.

Tactile Games

With all those mental gymnastics, your kid needs some mindless downtime to recover. Seasonal games are a lot of fun and can be very tactile too. Fall is a great time to make a leaf pile and let the kids jump around in it. It's like nature's sanitary version of a ball pit at a fast-food restaurant. And you don't even have to rake it.

Sense of Place is another tactile game. Most youngsters are visual learners, but this activity encourages them to use their other senses to have some fun and get to know their immediate surroundings. Play this game on a trail or in a grassy field or picnic area. It's a great game to play in a city park too. The seeker closes his eyes or puts on a blindfold while the guide spins the seeker around in a circle several times (if your child gets motion sickness, play this game *before* you eat a big meal). Of course the spinning is the silliest part of the game, so have fun with it (within reason!). Once the seeker is substantially disoriented, guide him to a feature in the forest or field—a tree, a wildflower, a shrub, a boulder, etc. When you arrive at the object, let the seeker touch, smell, and feel it for as long as he wants; then return the seeker to the exact spot where you started the game.

Now remove the blindfold and let the seeker try to identify the mystery object. This is a great way to get to know the different sizes of tree and plant leaves and the unique textures of tree bark, moss, and rocks. As a family, you'll notice that almost everything in the forest has distinct properties, much more so than if you played the same game at home with objects made of metal, plastic, or synthetics.

Speaking of home, if you're looking for a fun way to get your kids primed for a hike while also creating something fun to do while you're on the trail, consider a game of Trail Bingo. Brainstorm all the things you might see on your hike—squirrels, bugs, pinecones, different colored flowers or birds, varieties of trees or insects, water sources, etc. Then let everyone create his or her own bingo card (don't forget the free space in the middle—everybody loves a freebie) and determine a prize for the winner who cries out "Bingo!" first on the trail.

Arts and Crafts Time

Trail Bingo is a fun game, but if your 4-year-old isn't quite ready for such heated competition, never fear. There are gobs of other arts and crafts activities that fit right in on the trail. One of our favorites is to create nature prints of leaves, weeds, flowers, or anything else that's flat, interesting, and no longer alive. As long as you have pencils or crayons and some paper, and your kiddo has the dexterity to turn the drawing utensil sideways, making nature prints—or even a nature collage—can be an entertaining and educational art project that also makes a great gift for Grandma or Grandpa.

Drawing on rocks with water is a fun way to cool off on a hot summer day.
KAREN BOOTHE

If there are evergreens in your area, try some pinecone art. More sophisticated forms of pinecone art include holiday arrangements like wreaths or snowflakes. Or keep it simple and lighthearted by making snow owls with a bag of cotton balls or a turkey using construction paper and a few magic markers.

Here's one that blends engineering and imagination: Build a fairy or troll home. Broken sticks and small stones are the original form of Legos and Lincoln Logs, so all the materials you need to construct the home are right on the trail. Use fallen leaves for the roof or dead pine needles for a soft, comfortable carpet. Just be sure to collect *fallen* sticks rather than twigs and branches off living trees or shrubs. And try to gather small, loose stones rather than larger ones that could disturb an animal's habitat. To add to the fun, let the children make up a story about the troll or fairy who lives in the house. A fun way to pass on the joy? Leave the home intact in that spot on the trail for others to see. Just spotting a fairy house can brighten someone's day or do wonders for a child's imagination.

Animal Games

If you think you may have a future veterinarian on your hands, consider playing some animal games to nurture her love of critters. One simple activity we enjoy is to "listen like a deer." Have you ever seen deer listening intently when it senses danger is near? It rotates its ears in different directions like a satellite

dish. It's one of a deer's most important defense mechanisms. When we're on a hike, we like to listen in this way by cupping our hands next to our ears and swiveling them around. It's pretty remarkable how different things sound when you're listening in different directions. Go ahead and try it.

Another activity for the budding tracker is to figure out what kind of animal left a certain set of tracks or a pile of scat (animal poop). All you need to play this game is a notepad, pencil, magnifying glass, and sense of adventure. Set the scene by telling your child that he is going to be a detective for the day. Your goal is to figure out what animals walked on the trail. This game is especially fun after a rain or winter storm, because the mud and snow tend to create more obvious tracks.

When you see footprints, have your child measure them with a stick then trace them into his notebook. He can follow the tracks to determine where they lead and make notes about his observations. Do they disappear beside some berry bushes or at the base of a tree? If you have a magnifying glass, your child might be able to determine whether the animal has claws or not. Once he's recorded all the pertinent information, ask him some questions to

A Baker's Dozen of Tried-and-True Trail Activities

Here's a quick hit list of activities that completely rock on the trail:

1. **Climb a tree**—just make sure you can make it back down safely.

2. **Find a swimming hole.** One of Brew's favorite activities if he's near a glacial lake or stream is to take a "1-minute challenge" where he stays submerged for—you guessed it—at least a minute. His personal favorite (also his coldest) was a June soak in Crater Lake National Park when most of the park was still covered in snow.

3. **Search for bird nests.** But don't touch them, especially if there are eggs in there.

4. **Blow dandelions**—this is particularly fun for the little ones.

5. **Pack a fancy picnic lunch.** Visit your favorite grocery store and go all in with expensive charcuterie, designer cheeses, high-end olives, fresh fruit, cloth napkins, silver cutlery, crystal stemware, etc.

6. **Hunt for mushrooms and other edibles.** They're great in soups and teas, and some have healing properties. Just make sure you know what you're eating.

7. **Bring along a field guide** to identify flowers, birds, or trees.

8. **Pick wild berries** (but be sure you know what's edible and what's not!). Blueberries in August are our personal favorite. Bring an empty gallon milk jug with the top cut off to carry out your haul.

9. **Soak in a hot spring**—perfect after a long day of hiking.

10. **Volunteer as a trail maintainer.** This is a great way to give back and to learn about the landscape near you. Visit American Hiking Society (americanhiking.org) to find out more.

11. **Go for a trail run with the family.** You have to watch your footing, but it's a completely different way to experience the wilderness. And it's a welcome change from the car exhaust and red lights you face on a road run.

12. **Hug a tree!** Forget the politics. If you've never hugged a tree, just give it a try. Trust us: You'll feel better. And so will the tree.

13. **Go stargazing.** Trails are usually a *lot* better place for star gazing than neighborhoods are, provided you're not under a canopy of trees. So take a hike at night and get lost in the wonders of the galaxy. (You don't have to go too far to stargaze. Even stepping just outside the city limits will give you a clearer view of the sky.)

get his brain thinking: "How big do you think the animal is?" "What do you think it was doing?" "Was it walking, running, or hopping?" Finally, have your child guess what animal left the tracks.

Investigate scat in much the same way. It can tell you a lot about animals and the landscape in which they live, and since poop is already fascinating to kids, why not turn their feces fascination into something useful? Are any tracks leading to or from your discovery? Poke the poop with a stick to observe what's inside it. Often you will find berries, chewed-up leaves, seeds, and nuts. If the animal is a carnivore, you'll likely find some fur and bone fragments. Ask your child to record this information as well as the color, size, and shape of the poop. (Is it in pellets? A pile?) Your child might giggle or act disgusted, but he'll be entertained and also learn something. Once you have information on the scat and tracks you've encountered, pull out a trusty field guide to identify the animal. Or wait until you get home and look online. One great website that can provide loads of information before or after your hike is naturetracking.com.

MIDDLE SCHOOL

Preteens are not always keen on playing the same games as their younger siblings. But if you find an age-appropriate activity for your 12-year-old, chances are he or she will be entertained for hours and enjoy hiking even more.

Geocaching and Letterboxing

Geocaching—or digital treasure hunting in the woods—is the perfect game for pre-teens. To play, you'll need a GPS unit or a smartphone with a geocaching app that you can download for free. The basic app has most of the features a novice geocacher needs. Use your phone or GPS device to identify the geocaches (treasures) located in your area. When your GPS location matches up with the geocache position, start looking around for the indicated cache. Sometimes the item—often a simple prize in a plastic container to protect it from the elements—will be in plain view; other times it will be camouflaged, and you have to look hard to locate it. If you can't find the item with the naked eye, check the app to see if there's a clue to its whereabouts in the description.

Geocaching is a fun way to engage your middle schooler.
©THINKSTOCK.COM/PIXIECLOUD

Regardless of the shape and size, finding a geocache is always a treat. Bring a pen to record your visit in the cache's register. You can also record comments on the geocaching app or website to connect with and assist fellow geocache seekers.

Geocaching is a great activity for families to enjoy on the trail, but you can also have fun looking for these treasures in city parks and urban settings, making it the perfect activity for you urban dwellers out there. You can even participate in geocaching by planting your own weatherproof container with a note and small journal in any area with public access. For more about geo-caching, check out geocaching.com.

If you like geocaching but don't want your daughter staring at her smart-phone for your entire hike, consider letterboxing. Letterboxing is also great for younger kids. It's similar to geocaching, except the searcher can print out clues from online letterboxing sites and create a scavenger hunt for the hidden treasure. The largest collection of clues can be found at letter boxing.org.

Trail Mix

One of the tastiest and easiest camp stove creations to make with your family on an overnight trip or extended day hike is a mini pizza. The ingredients are simple, the cooking time is quick, and the finished product is delectable.

Mini Pizzas

1 package 4.5-inch flour tortillas (or English muffins)

1 14-ounce jar pizza sauce

1 8-ounce bag shredded mozzarella cheese

Pizza toppings of your choosing (pepperoni, precooked bacon, chopped peppers, onions, mushrooms, olives, etc.)

Gear: Camp stove, fuel, pocketknife, and a 5-inch nonstick frying pan with handle or cooking clamps

Place a flour tortilla into the fry pan and spread a layer of sauce on it. (If you don't have a nonstick pan, pack butter or oil to grease the surface before cooking.) Allow your child to sprinkle cheese on top then decorate with toppings. Don't be afraid to turn this into an art project. Make a smiley face or other design on your pizza. Or see if you prefer Chicago style (with sauce on top) to New York style (with cheese on top).

Put the pizza in the pan and cook it over medium heat. The pizza is done when the edges of the crust turn brown and the cheese has melted. If the flour tortilla starts to burn, reduce the flame or manually hold the pan higher over the burner.

Allow the pizza to cool for a couple minutes. This meal is eaten and served in rounds, so you might want to combine mealtime with another form of entertainment mentioned in this chapter.

Letterboxers search for containers—think an old cigar box or a metal tin—that house unique stamps and a passbook. When you find a letterbox, you mark your own notebook with the unique stamp that's inside, kind of like how you get your passport stamped in a foreign country. But here's what's cool—you carry a unique stamp with you that's your own personal calling card. You leave *your* stamp in the letterbox logbook so that people know you've been there.

Campground Olympics

If you have a particularly sporty or competitive family on your hands, consider holding your first ever Family Campground Olympics. Devise your Olympiad at home, or see what you come up with on the trail. Can you find eight big stones and one small one? Then you've got yourself a game of campground bocce ball. Is your tent site surrounded by a creek, a bunch of rocks, or some fallen trees? Create an obstacle course and see who can make it through the fastest. Collect pinecones and see which team can get the most catches without a drop. Find out who can skip a rock the farthest or make the biggest cannon-ball into the swimming hole or, in the fall, who can catch the most leaves in 60 seconds. Choose teams, organize opening and closing ceremonies, and create awards. Use your imagination. And be sure to bring your "A" game.

©ISTOCK.COM/ESOKOLOVSKAYA

HIGH SCHOOL

We've worked with dozens of high school groups over the years, and almost all of them have loved engaging in lighthearted activities on the trail. Most teens welcome the chance to be a kid again and see games as a diversion from the busyness of their everyday lives. That said, we are not *related* to these teens, and sometimes kids put a barrier up with their parents that they don't put up for other adults. Besides, some teens just feel as though they have enough structure at school and with their extracurriculars, so they're not interested in having "required fun" on the trail, regardless of whether parents are involved or not. To them the word "game" sounds like something for their little sister, and "activities" conjure up images of a field trip for science class. Regardless of where your teen falls on the spectrum, it's a good idea to keep a few activities up your sleeve that you can offer up in a covert, "hip parent" kind of way.

There are plenty of opportunities on the trail for your teenager to have fun—and crack a smile again.
DAVIS FAMILY

Survivor Kid

If your son or daughter is into construction, engineering, or survival skills, consider building a primitive shelter together. If your hometown gets a lot of snowfall in winter, research how to build an igloo and, if you're feeling really adventuresome (and warm-blooded), spend the night in it. But even if it's not winter and you don't live in a cold-weather climate, there are many different types of lean-tos and shelters you can build with just dirt, leaves, and fallen limbs.

Before you head out, go over different types of shelters with your son or daughter and discuss the models that are best suited for your region. Visit wilderness-survival.net for a great list of these structures with pictures and instructions on how to build them.

Gear up for your adventure by watching Bear Grylls or another survival show together. The theatrics and camerawork on those shows are so entertaining that you may want to use your smartphone or GoPro to record your own survival experience. Your teen will have fun showing his survival experience to his friends. And his primitive skills will come in handy if he ever has to flee the big city because of a zombie apocalypse.

Same Word, Different Song

If your teen is tuned into his ear buds and you're looking for a way to make the hike more interactive, consider suggesting this back-and-forth singing competition. It is a great way to incorporate music into your hike and compare songs from different generations.

The rules of the game are simple. To start, one person needs to sing a line or two from a song he or she knows. When the first person is finished, the next takes a word or phrase from the song lyrics just recited and sings a different song that includes the same word or phrase. (If you've ever seen the movie *Pitch Perfect*, they call this a "riff-off.") You can play with as many people as you have on the trail. The catch is that you have to start your new song within 30 seconds or you're out of the game.

The best part is that by playing with your kids, you're likely to hear songs that you never knew existed. Likewise, your kids will be astonished—if not mortified—at your inventory of "oldies." You'll almost certainly start laughing at some of the more soulful renditions. And when it's all over, you might even find yourself downloading some Usher.

One more version of a riff-off is something we like to call "The Spelling Game." (Pretty creative, eh?) One person starts off by saying a letter, and the next person has to add a second letter to the first without spelling a word. Whoever does spell a word is out. For example, if the first letter is "O," the second person wouldn't want to say "F" because that spells "of." Instead,

real story

A Kid's Perspective

I've been on the trail since I was a baby. We have pictures of me in a backpack carrier hiking in Alaska at 4 months old. Now I am 11 and still on the trail. The trail means a lot to me and my family, and many other people too. We are all nature lovers. And for people like my family and me, that suits us fine.

Little bloopers on the trail are sometimes funny, other times not. But one way or another they teach lessons. My family went on a hike with our dog. She's crazy around people. She sniffs everybody and then jumps on them. It's embarrassing. Once on a hike she pooped in the middle of the busy path. We had to wait for everyone to pass us so no one stepped on it.

My family and I have a list of steps we take before getting on the trail:

1. We get all the appropriate clothes out for the hike. We check the forecast for that day and get clothes out accordingly.

2. We each fill our backpacks with a water bottle, a raincoat (if chance of rain), a hat (in all seasons), sunscreen, a snack (granola bar, trail mix, etc.), bug spray, and a GPS.

3. We gather all our stuff, jump in the car, and away we go.

Sometimes we are bored on the trail, but my sister and I walk up to the front of the line and pick up all the sticks (1 to 3 feet in length) we can find. Then we pick the two biggest and use those as our hiking sticks. Those little joys on the trail are what make hiking so fun. I encourage anyone interested in hiking to try it out. You will be amazed at what you discover.

—Stephanie Hoffarth, age 11,
Sheyenne River Valley Chapter,
North Country Trail Association

Stephanie Hoffarth with a family member
COURTESY STEPHANIE HOFFARTH

Older children love scrambling over rocks too.
SHAWN PERCHALUK

she might say "P" because "op" isn't a word. The third person might say "E" as opposed to "T," because "ope" isn't a word but "opt" is. If the next person can't think of a word besides one that would put her out (say, "open") or thinks the preceding person doesn't actually have a word, she can challenge. But if the third person does have a word in mind—say, "operate"—the challenger is outta there. Bonus: This is a sneaky way to get your teen to review for those dreaded standardized tests.

Hiking Murder Mystery

If your family is into theatrics (let's be honest, what teen *isn't* into drama?), consider a murder mystery game on the trail. This activity passes the time on lengthy hikes and allows your kids to use their imagination and acting skills. You need a minimum of four people to make this game work, but it's even better with six to eight participants. So it's a perfect game when your teen invites some friends along for the trip.

Murder mysteries require a little work on the front end. Familiarize yourself with a plot, and jot down character descriptions on notecards at home. You can find plenty of free murder mystery scenarios online. The website freeformgames.com even has a list of plots specifically for teens. Or check out free murder mysteries for smaller groups at 411party.com. Start with a prescripted mystery, but if you're a creative type and pick up on it quickly, you may want to create your own.

If you're not into the whole acting thing, riddles and whodunits are a great way to pass the time and keep your family engaged on a day hike or around the campfire. One of our favorite online resources is 5minutemystery.com. When they're in groups, teens seem to really love problem solving because they can feed off one another with their line of questioning. We've spent 45 minutes trying to solve a single riddle with some groups; inevitably, once they figure out the first one, they can't wait to tackle more.

But let's say your teen isn't into the deductive reasoning of riddles, either. Well good old-fashioned ghost stories can be loads of fun too. Flashlights, headlamps, and the flicker of the flame set the perfect stage for scaring cocksure teens out of their wits. And it certainly brings their attention to nocturnal sights and sounds they otherwise may not notice. That said, if you've got *younger* children around, you may not want to engage in these potentially hair-raising activities unless you're ready for them to snuggle up next to you in the wee hours of the morning. For that matter, you may not want to spook teens or adults either if they're backpacking novices who are already having trouble adjusting to the trail at night. Just know your audience and plan accordingly.

Arts and Crafts

If your teen has a gift for the arts, you may not need to do anything more than get him on the trail and turn him loose before he's blown away by the inspiration that lies before him. Smartphones and GoPros are perfect tools for the would-be photographer, cinematographer, or documentarian. If you really want to blow his mind, give your teen an old-fashioned camera with film—say an 8 millimeter or an SLR. Just be sure he knows not to take hundreds of photos in the first 5 minutes, because those photos can't be deleted, and prints cost money to develop.

For the aspiring landscape artist, pencils, paper, and watercolors fit easily into a day pack. And visual arts aren't the only form of creativity in the wilderness. Nature has always been a muse for authors, songwriters, and composers too, and the teenage years are the perfect time for your child to hone his skills in these disciplines. One of our friends is a songwriter who also happens to be a terrific trail runner. Every time he goes on a run, he snaps a few photos with his iPhone and writes a simple haiku to post on Facebook. Some are funny and some are beautiful, but all of them are inspired by nature, and they're a great way to keep his creative juices flowing. All these artistic endeavors are fantastic on-trail activities because they allow your teen to be near the group while also exercising independence and individualism. And really, that's what the teenage years are all about: giving your children roots to know that they're loved and that you'll always be there for them, while also giving them wings to explore and become their own person.

next step

If your family has a favorite board game or other activity, bring it on the trail with you. Nothing is off limits. If it fits in your pack, is something everyone is familiar with, and makes your kids feel more at home on the trail, by all means bring it along. Some of our go-to comfort activities for keeping Charley entertained include crayons, coloring books, regular books, and—her personal favorite—bubbles. As for our source of evening entertainment, small games that travel light are best—think Banana-grams, Travel Scrabble, or a deck of cards.

Here's a list of potential go-to comfort items and activities:

☐ Favorite stuffed animal, action figure, or other small toy
☐ Dog-eared book
☐ Coloring book and crayons
☐ Travel board games (often in smaller formats than the at-home versions)
☐ Jigsaw puzzles (if you're going to be somewhere with a picnic table or other flat surface)
☐ Dress-up costumes

learn

chapter 7

Learning, Conserving, Volunteering

Whenever I play around the house with Charley, she's always ready to move on to the next activity after a little while. What starts with painting jungle creatures in the dining room with paper, brushes, and acrylics turns into story time, with every book pulled off her bookshelf and strewn throughout the house. And it ends playing "pretend mommy," and I am somehow tucked away on the couch in the living room under mounds of her stuffed animals and her bed comforter.

By the time Jen tags in to take over, and I get a chance to take stock of everything, a toddler tornado has ripped through our house. And it happens so quickly and effortlessly. We aren't *trying* to make a mess; we are just doing our thing. But we destroy—*destroy*—our living space.

So what does this have to do with hiking? Recently I spent a few days on the Appalachian Trail in northeast Tennessee. It was peak "thru-hiker" season, and while I was out there I was struck by how much trash was lying around. Most of it was in streams near the trailheads or at road crossings, but even in the backcountry I saw cellophane wrappers, wool socks hanging from tree branches, and plastic bottle caps stuck in the mud.

We aren't *trying* to make a mess on the trail; we're just doing our thing. But our intention doesn't change the bottom line, which is that we're having an impact. And it's important for us to realize that, because until we do, we're not going to make a concerted effort to clean stuff up, either in one fell swoop on a volunteer cleanup day or a little at a time by picking up the occasional empty chip bag or tent stake along the trail.

One bumper sticker I see quite often says, "Do No Harm." That's certainly a good place to start, but if you ask me, it doesn't go far enough. Instead, I think it should say, "Do Some Good." Groups like Leave No Trace are doing

Hiking trail in Gila Wilderness, New Mexico
©THINKSTOCK.COM/DESIGN PICS

just that—and making it easy for you too to participate—by having designated cleanup days throughout the year.

We did our best to keep this chapter succinct because nobody wants to read a laundry list of trail do's and don'ts. For my part, I know that I'd rather spend my day walking down the trail than cleaning it up, but I also know that at some point I need to pick up after myself. And that I need to teach Charley to do the same.

—Brew Davis

PRESERVING OUR ENVIRONMENT

Earth's population today is between seven and eight billion people. But did you know that in your children's lifetime that number will increase by about 50 percent? That's a staggering figure. And it's a bit daunting when you consider that there's a finite amount of Earth's most basic resources available, like arable land and clean drinking water.

If we want our children to conserve and preserve those resources, it's *really* important that we expose them to hiking trails and wild places. The reality is that most of us don't think about protecting things we haven't experienced. It's not that we don't care; it's just not in the forefront of our minds. If we want our kids to value wilderness in all its uniqueness and beauty, we have to give them an emotional connection to it.

Encourage your kids to interact with wildlife; just make sure they use gentle hands.
DAVIS FAMILY

There are dozens of ways to give back to the trails and, in turn, take care of the environment. This chapter covers age-appropriate ways to give back and to implement Leave No Trace ethics while on your family hikes. We'll also discuss the basics of hiker etiquette.

But while etiquette and ethics are important, don't turn into a trail gestapo. A hike with your family shouldn't feel restrictive. If you see someone else not doing the right thing, do your best to balance Leave No Trace ethics with a desire to leave your fellow hiker with a positive trail experience. Ultimately, keeping these principles in mind should give you confidence to know what you can and can't do, which in turn allows you to have the most fun and safe adventure possible.

PRESCHOOL

It can be daunting to teach your toddler—you know, the one who can't keep her room clean for more than 5 minutes—how to properly care for the environment. But small habits implemented at a young age make a big difference as your child matures.

Typically your children will not toss trash or biodegradable items like apple cores to the side of the trail unless they see their parents model that behavior. Although an apple core tossed in a native setting biodegrades faster than a banana peel or orange rind, which surprisingly can take up to two years to biodegrade (it takes 250 to 500 million years for a disposable diaper to decompose!), *pack it out*, no matter how messy.

Even a lone apple core will attract wild animals to the trail, animals that associate human activity with food waste. That connection proves harmful to both people and animals. The same holds true for when you spill a little trail mix on the side of the path—and with a small child, you *will* spill trail mix. Clean as much of it up as possible before you leave so that you don't invite wild animals to graze on the side of the trail.

With food and all other hiking items, it's always best to teach your children that if you pack it in, you

"If you pack it in, you also need to pack it out."

We have to properly care for the environment to ensure that generations after us get to enjoy it like we do.
KATIE CARDOSO

Hiking Etiquette and Leave No Trace Principles

Before starting a hike, you should familiarize yourself with these hiking etiquette basics from American Hiking Society and Leave No Trace principles.

American Hiking Society's Guidelines for Proper Hiking Etiquette

Guiding Principle: Be respectful of the land and other hikers.

- Hike quietly. Speak in low voices and turn your cell phone down, if not off. Enjoy the sounds of nature, and let others do the same.
- If taking a break, move off the trail a ways to allow others to pass by unobstructed.
- Don't toss your trash—not even biodegradable items such as banana peels. It is not good for animals to eat nonnative foods, and who wants to look at your old banana peel while it ever so slowly decomposes? If you packed it in, pack it back out.
- Hikers going downhill yield to those hiking uphill.
- When bringing a pet on a hike, be sure to keep it on a leash and under control. Don't forget to pack out pet waste as well.
- Don't feed the wildlife. While many animals stay hidden, others are not so shy. Giving these creatures food only disrupts their natural foraging habits.
- Leave what you find. The only souvenirs a hiker should come home with are photographs and happy memories. (And maybe an improved fitness level!)
- When relieving yourself outdoors, be sure to do so 200 feet away from the trail and any water sources. Follow Leave No Trace principles.
- Walk through the mud or puddle, not around it, unless you can do so without going off the trail. Widening a trail by going around puddles, etc., is bad for trail sustainability. Just because it looks easy to cut the corner off of a switchback doesn't mean it is a good idea. Help preserve the trail by staying on the trail.
- If hiking in a group, don't take up the whole width of the trail; allow others to pass.

Leave No Trace Principles

(The following list was created by the Leave No Trace organization and is supported and implemented by American
Hiking Society. You'll probably notice some overlap.)

*Guiding Principle: "Leave what you find, take only photos and
memories."*

1. Plan ahead and prepare. Know the type of terrain and
   weather conditions you might encounter. Minimize impacts
   by keeping groups small and avoiding high use times for
   the trail. Walking single file and avoiding shortcuts will limit
   damage to the trail and surrounding ecosystems.
2. Travel and camp on durable surfaces. Focus activity on
   resilient ground. Surfaces consisting of sand, gravel, rock,
   snow, or dry grass are durable and can withstand heavy
   use. Walk through mud/puddles to avoid widening the trail.
3. Dispose of waste properly. Pack it in, pack it out! This includes not only
   food wrappers, but also biodegradable waste such as banana peels, etc.
   Also practice "negative trace" by picking up trash left by others. Dispose of
   human waste in catholes dug 6–8 inches deep in soil at least 200 feet from
   any water source. Pack out all toilet paper and hygiene products.
4. Leave what you find. You can look, but please don't take. Leave everything
   that you find in the wilderness where it belongs. Avoid moving rocks, picking
   plants, and disturbing cultural or historical artifacts.
5. Minimize campfire impacts. Keep your campfire small—or go without. Use
   previously constructed fire rings or mounds. Only burn small-diameter wood
   found on the ground. Do not damage live or fallen trees. Be aware of the
   level of fire danger of the area. Make sure your campfire is completely smothered before you leave camp. Small camping stoves are much more efficient
   for cooking, and leave no impact on the site.
6. Respect wildlife. Let the wild be wild. Keep your distance and do not attract
   or approach animals. Never feed them food intended for humans, as this disrupts their natural foraging habits. Control pets in natural areas, and always
   keep them restrained.
7. Be considerate of other visitors. Show respect for other trail users. Keep
   noise from getting intrusively loud. Obey any posted trail rules, including
   rights-of-way. Orient rest spots and campsites away from the trail. Attempt to
   minimize visual impacts by wearing clothes that are earth-tone colors (unless,
   of course, hiking in the vicinity of hunters): brown, green, tan, or black.

For more on Leave No Trace principles, visit their website: LeaveNoTrace.org.

Mountain laurel in full bloom
DAVIS FAMILY

also need to pack it out. And once your kids get the hang of this principle, model even better behavior by picking up and packing out small pieces of litter. Even picking up two or three gum wrappers or a lost shoestring can have an impact. Just think of how clean the trails would be if every hiker picked up a scrap of litter or two every time he or she took a hike. Incidentally, those extra plastic zip and grocery bags, or even the packaging you used for dinner, can make for great trash receptacles.

Flora and Fauna

It is also important to model healthy behaviors for picking vegetation. Again, keeping things in perspective here is key. We won't split hairs over picking a dandelion or three in a field full of them, but it's good to teach your child to leave a lone wildflower alone so that other hikers can enjoy its beauty too.

Another topic of debate—especially with young children—is how to engage with wildlife. We've mentioned wildlife before and there's certainly no consensus. Some hikers say all animals should be left alone and disturbed as little as possible by humans. Others argue that catching fireflies, looking for salamanders, and petting toads are some of the best ways for children and adults to have a potentially life-changing encounter with nature. Regardless of your stance, show consideration for animals and don't remove them from their natural habitat. If you see a critter that looks like it's injured, chances are it's just resting. Even if it's not, you may do more harm than good trying to help it. If you're really concerned, alert a park office or a ranger, and let them take it from there.

Similarly, you may come across an animal that seems lost or abandoned. A lot of times mommas leave their young while they run out to the grocery store to grab lunch. It's best

Some kids are tree huggers—and some are tree kissers.
MICHELLE BAILEN

Stay on the trail, even when it's hard to find.
©THINKSTOCK.COM/OMGIMAGES

Trail Mix

If all this talk about Leave No Trace and reducing your impact on the trail has inspired you to reduce your environmental footprint at home too, one of the best ways to do it is to eat local, organic produce. When local fruits and veggies are in season, they make a perfect trail snack. One way to enjoy local produce in a portable, trail-friendly way is to make fruit strips at home.

Besides being easy to carry, fruit strips are loaded with nutrients and bursting with flavor. They also happen to be a great way to preserve fruit and stockpile health snacks for a later date. Three cheers for tricking your kids into eating something healthy!

Fruit Strips

2 cups chopped local fruit (some of the best choices are peaches, apricots, apples, strawberries, blueberries, blackberries, raspberries, or pears)*

1 cup water

1 teaspoon lemon juice

2 teaspoons honey

*Feel free to mix and match, especially if you use juicy fruits, like citrus or melon. If you are feeling adventurous, throw in some local veggies too. If you're like us, you probably won't want to disclose these ingredients to your children right away.

Preheat the oven to 150°F. Place the chopped fruit in a cooking pan and add 1 cup water. Cook on medium heat until the fruit is soft. Remove the pan from the stove; allow the mixture to cool then pour into a blender. Add lemon juice and honey then puree until smooth.

Line a baking sheet with parchment paper and pour the puree on top. Place in the oven and cook for 4 or 5 hours, depending on how tough you want your fruit strips. If you like softer strips, remove when puree is slightly sticky. For a chewier snack, remove when completely dry to the touch.

Once your creation cools to room temperature, make strips with a pizza cutter. Test out a few strips. Wrap up the rest and you'll be good to go for your next hike.

to leave those critters alone. Most animals have a sixth sense that more or less prevents them from getting lost. So it's better not to get involved in their business.

One particularly relevant Leave No Trace principle for parents with toddlers is to teach your kids to stay on durable surfaces, whether dirt, rock, bog logs, or something else. You don't need to belabor the point; all you really have to say is, "Stay on the trail." This keeps your kids safe and also keeps the trail in good shape.

No one wants muddy feet (well, maybe your toddler does), but if you see standing water or puddles interspersed with shoe-sucking mud, walk through them. It may seem harmless to climb up on the shoulder of the trail, but doing this ultimately wears away the edge and makes the puddle bigger. If you're really concerned about getting your feet wet, lay some sticks down to create a makeshift bridge. Eventually, trail maintainers should come along and fix the problem, but until they do, it's best not to walk around the edges.

You may come across boardwalks on your hike, especially in more urban locations. When given the option to walk the boardwalk or hop down and tread on the grass, remember that the boardwalk is there

Admire the beauty around you, but remember to leave it as you found it.
DAVIS FAMILY

for a reason. Sometimes it's to keep the environment safe from humans, and sometimes it is the other way around. Several years ago we took a hike through Jean Lafitte National Historical Park and Preserve in New Orleans. Much of the hike was on boardwalk, despite the ground looking hard and firm. But in other places it passed through swampland thick with vegetation. We passed dozens of small water snakes in this section. They didn't seem venomous, but we were very happy to be on that boardwalk several feet off the ground.

ELEMENTARY SCHOOL

Your toddler will most likely be comfortable peeing and pooping on the trail by himself. In fact, it's a great place to work on potty training because, for the most part, your kiddo can *wilderness pee*—as our daughter likes to say— whenever and wherever he wants. But you're probably still helping him with his business at that point and—ahem—handling his used toilet paper.

By elementary school, your older children should be able to go to the bathroom unassisted—and unabashed. Woohoo! So with that in mind, elementary school is the sweet spot for teaching kids how to go to the bathroom properly on a hike too. Do yourself and your kid a favor, and don't just send him off to the "men's tree" with a trowel, toilet paper, plastic bag, and hand sanitizer. Make sure he knows how to use everything so that he doesn't, well, make a mess. So here goes:

The proper place to poop in the woods is 200 feet from trails, campsites, and water sources (think two-thirds of a football field). Your 7-year-old might need a little help here. Don't send him out of eyesight; instead, walk off-trail with him a ways then let him go a bit farther to find some privacy behind a tree or a rock. (Most hikers won't go this far away from a campsite or trail if they just have to tinkle, but it's still important to keep this distance from water sources.)

For number two, dig a 6- to 8-inch "cat hole" with a trowel (a small, lightweight digging tool). If you don't have a trowel, use a stick, a hiking pole, or a pointed rock. Do your best to leave all your waste in the hole, then cover it up with dirt. If you use toilet paper and bury it, it will eventually decompose. But if it's not too messy, the best thing to do is to wrap it in a plastic bag and pack it out.

Whether used or unused, never leave toilet paper lying on the ground, on a rock, or stuck in a bush. It's true that it doesn't decompose as fast when it's buried, but it also doesn't attract other animals down there—and it isn't gross for other hikers to look at. No one wants to see little TP flowers strewn about the forest floor.

On that note . . . ladies, you don't *have* to use toilet paper when you tinkle. It's a luxury, not a necessity. Next time you hike, plan on packing out your used refuse; better yet, give drip-drying a try.

When washing up, use hand sanitizer, a key item for day hikes and overnights. Soap isn't the best thing for lakes and streams—not even the all-natural variety. After you go to the bathroom, just squirt a little sanitizer on your palms and be on your way.

Eventually you and your family might enjoy using the on-trail restroom. After all, it has far fewer germs than any public restroom you have ever visited.

Save the Earth: Destroy Stuff!

What elementary schooler doesn't love destroying stuff? One way you can put this natural predilection to good use *and* help the environment is by deconstructing illegal fire rings and campsites. Talk to a park ranger or trail maintainer before undertaking this project, but typically they will be more than happy to tell you where illegal or "stealth" campsites have popped up. Usually

Don't let your kids off so easy—put them to work covering up stealth campsites.
SHARON BRODIN

land agencies want to limit tenting to official or preestablished areas so that there aren't endless clearings with fire rings and sitting logs along the trail.

If you get permission to cover a stealth site, the objective is to make it look like no one has spent the night there, which means you get to take advantage of one of your children's greatest skills—making a mess! Before starting, inspect the area to make doubly sure there are no hot coals simmering. Disassemble the fire ring by throwing the rocks into the woods (not *at* one another). Then use a fallen branch—preferably with a tuft of leaves—to spread out the ashes.

Next up, roll any logs that look as though they've been used to sit on as far away from the fire pit as possible. If you can't roll them, you can always spin them sideways so they no longer make a circle. Finally, spread as much debris as possible—sticks, dead leaves, pinecones, pine needles, fallen branches, even small dead trees—around to disguise the former site from would-be campers. The only caveat here is that this project will most definitely give your kids experience in covering their own tracks when they've been up to no good.

MIDDLE SCHOOL

When I taught middle school, I decided that my job wasn't *quite* crazy enough, so I started an afterschool hiking group. I named it the Cougar Mountain Club for the school's mascot. Over the course of the semester, the group covered almost 30 continuous miles along the Mountains-to-Sea Trail that makes a crescent around Asheville, North Carolina. Once or twice Jen tagged along on these outings and was struck by how these kids—mostly sixth-grade boys— seemed more like a pride of wild lions or bear cubs than middle schoolers. Those little Tasmanian devils laughed, hiked, and tussled along in a cloud of dust on the trail.

The kids in the Cougar Mountain Club were no different from most middle school students. When they weren't completely rebooting their brains and getting out loads of excess energy, they were off in their own worlds, wrapped up in their own thoughts. I once saw a boy literally walk straight into a tree. He

Nature at its best, and most beautiful: Rocky Mountains
DAVIS FAMILY

later admitted that he had been thinking about a difficult stage on his favorite video game.

The point is this: Middle schoolers have a *lot* of energy, and they can also be an absent-minded bunch. These are actually *great* reasons to get your kids on the trail. But if they are not under control, it can also spell disaster for other unsuspecting hikers. It's important to remind them regularly to be considerate of others. If your kids career past you on a down-hill as an elderly couple hikes slowly and steadily toward you, your kids need to know to stop so that the couple moving can keep going. The trail is no different from basic physics: Objects in motion tend to stay in motion, because it's a lot harder to get going again on an uphill than it is to let gravity carry you down.

As middle schoolers grow more comfortable on the trail, they are tempted to cut corners on the "switchbacks" that go up and down hills and mountains. Other hikers may have created these shortcuts, and it may seem like a good idea for a tired parent or an energetic kid. But the problem is that these social paths, as they're called, erode the landscape and cause problems for trail builders and maintainers. So make sure your tween takes the extra 15 or 20 steps to where the trail makes its turn. If you see a stray limb or two, lay it over the improper trail so that others know where not to go. Besides, if your spark-plug sixth grader cuts corners, it's going to be even harder for you to keep up.

This is a good time to talk about durable versus nondurable surfaces. Durable surfaces—exposed sturdy areas—are better for walking than the non-durable surfaces (delicate vegetation areas). If you decide to picnic at a rock outcropping, for example, encourage your kids to keep their feet on the exposed rock as much as possible so they don't accidentally kill delicate vegetation—like lichen, moss, or flowers—growing between the cracks in the rock face.

For you coastal hikers, the same goes for hikes on sandy shorelines. Encourage your family to walk on hard-packed sand near the water instead of

Trail Tech

Scientific Apps

Several apps allow hikers to collect on-trail recordings to pass along to experts in the scientific community. "What's Invasive" is a free app from the University of Georgia designed to help record and monitor the spread of invasive exotic species on public land. You can see which exotic plants and insects are on-trail in your area and upload your sightings with your specific GPS coordinates. The app helps land management agencies control the spread of invasive exotic plants that are harmful to native habitats. And if you have a future botanist on your hands, it can turn your hike into a wilderness scavenger hunt.

iNaturalist records plant or animal encounters on the trail and uploads them to the iNaturalist community, which provides additional information on sightings. Data from this app is also shared with scientists, who then use your information to further their field research, thus making it possible for amateurs to participate in scientific discovery and, in some cases, contribute to meaningful breakthroughs.

real story

Trail Expectations

Little Emery gets ready to look for marbles on Marble Falls Trail.
TRISH ADAMS

It was early spring and my granddaughter, Emery, was 2½ years old. We were beginning preparations for her first "big kid" hike. She was getting to hike the entire time instead of riding in the backpack carrier. As we always do, we talked about where we would hike. I told her our trail choices were Ladybug Trail, Tokopah Falls Trail, and the Marble Falls Trail, all in Sequoia National Park.

Emery is very literal, as most children are at this age. She asked if there were ladybugs on Ladybug Trail. I told her yes, that there are hundreds of ladybugs on Ladybug Trail. She asked if there were falls on Tokopah Falls Trail. I told her yes, but they might still be mostly frozen. Finally, she asked if there were marbles on Marble Falls Trail. This question shouldn't have surprised me, but it did. I told her that we would see marble, like pretty white rocks, when we reached the end of the trail at the waterfall.

Hearing what she wanted to hear, she immediately cast her vote for the Marble Falls Trail. She told me that maybe we would see more marbles while we hiked on the trail. While we didn't find any marbles while hiking, we definitely had fun looking for them.

—Trish Adams

climbing on sand dunes or walking through sensitive vegetation like sea oats and saw grass. Those plants get hammered enough by the elements; the last thing they need to contend with is the feet of some overly enthusiastic middle schoolers. And if your kids love climbing over dead trees, be careful of poisonous plants and avoid mushrooms and other living things that feed off the decaying wood.

Save the Earth: Destroy Stuff

Consider having your preteen help a trail club remove invasive exotic plants from public lands or private nature preserves. Invasive plants spread quickly; exotic plants are those nonnative to the region where you live. Invasive exotics can be extremely harmful to the natural landscape. One example of an invasive exotic that has plagued the Southeast for decades is kudzu. This hearty, aggressive vine covers entire canopies and prevents low-lying native trees and shrubs from receiving the sunlight and nutrients they need to thrive, which in turn impacts the soil quality and the surrounding ecosystem. Kudzu can be removed by digging up the roots and severing the plant beneath the bulbous-looking collection of nodes (called the root crown), which is found just under the earth's surface.

Removing invasive exotics usually involves putting on gloves and using tools like a lopper, a hoe, and large garden scissors. It's hard work; but it's also a great outlet for all that preteen energy, there are tangible results, and it really helps the environment. Besides, what preteen you know wouldn't *love* taking out their pent-up aggression on some unsuspecting plants with a giant pair of garden scissors?

HIGH SCHOOL

If you're just introducing your teens to life on the trail, go over Leave No Trace ethics and trail etiquette principles with them (see the Leave No Trace section earlier in this chapter). But if you've been teaching them what to do all along, they should have a firm grasp of the basics and should even be able to share those concepts with less knowledgeable friends and siblings. The Leave No Trace website (lnt.org/teach/tools-and-activities-educators) offers downloadable slideshows and printouts, as well as instructional games and activities.

Even if your teens are well versed in trail ethics and Leave No Trace principles, there are still plenty of ways to expand their knowledge and explore the field. If your daughter happens to enjoy science or has a school fair coming up, she may want to put together an experiment to determine the rates of decomposition for different materials, for instance. Minus Styrofoam, which never decomposes, even the simplest materials like toilet paper and fruit peels

Single track isn't the only way to enjoy a great hike: Old roads and railroad beds can be just as scenic.
MP (MEGAN PETERSON) PHOTOGRAPHY

can take weeks or even months. She could even explore variables such as aboveground decomposition versus belowground or wet conditions versus dry.

If your teen is interested in conservation and preservation but prefers writing more than scientific research, he may want to apply for an internship with a land advocacy or policy group. Organizations like the Sierra Club and The Nature Conservancy have offices across the country, but there are also regional-specific groups that have an impact on state and local law. For example, a vital organization in our neck of the woods is the Southern Environmental Law Center, which has offices scattered across the Southeast. There are also local nonprofits that fight for conservation and preservation efforts in almost every city and county across the nation.

We've just touched on the brainier side of conservation, but there are plenty of on-trail opportunities that allow high schoolers to get their hands dirty. And some of the most important ones don't require any knowledge of Leave No Trace principles. By now, all teens know that trash doesn't belong on trails or in streambeds. If your son's high school has a service club or a day designated for service projects, he can pick up trash along a segment of trail or in a streambed. Earlier, we mentioned that younger kids can dismantle illegal campsites and extricate invasive exotic plants—and teens who are willing to work hard should be able to "clean house" more effectively than your younger kids.

Volunteer Trail Crews and Internships

Summer is a great time for kids to volunteer on a trail crew. Trail crews typically spend a week or two in the backcountry, maintaining and improving trail systems by building water bars, moving heavy rocks, cutting up trees that have fallen in storms, creating steps to reduce erosion, and removing invasive exotic plants. It's exhausting just writing about it. But the combination of manual labor plus engineering may be just what your teen loves. And when you throw in the opportunity to spend time with a group of like-minded peers in a beautiful setting, the experience really is life-changing. Besides, it's pretty much guaranteed that if your teen participates in a work crew, he will never cut a switchback or sidestep a mud puddle again.

Consider volunteering for a trail crew together as parent and child. There may be no better way for you and your teen to bond than to spend a week away from work and school, away from telephones and TV, away from friends and other family members, simply working together side by side in the wilderness.

On the other hand, if you and your teen need some space from each other, or if she is eager to invest more than just a week or two, she may want to apply for an internship. The National Parks Service has hundreds of them. The Student Conservation Association organizes programs year-round and has two branches—Public Lands Corps and Youth Conservation Corps—that offer summer-specific programs. Besides being a terrific volunteer opportunity and a résumé builder for college applications, these internships are also a great way for young people to get their foot in the door if they're considering a career with NPS or the federal government's Department of the Interior.

Whether on a trail in Idaho's Sawtooth National Forest or in an office near the Capitol in Washington, DC, *hard work* has been the essence of conservation and preservation for more than a century; the same is true going forward. The NPS and similar state and city agencies have had consistent budget cuts for years and need billions of dollars to get their infrastructure up to speed. So if our children want to have trails to hike on and wild places to enjoy, it's important that we engender a culture of service and volunteerism by pitching in whenever and wherever we can.

next step

Leave No Trace Certification

If you or anyone in your family is interested in learning more about Leave No Trace, there are great learning opportunities available. Currently, Leave No Trace has four teams of traveling trainers who offer workshops in different regions of the United States to educate and motivate Leave No Trace practices.

☐ *Visit the Leave No Trace website (lnt.org), or check in with your local outdoor store to see if trainers are scheduled to visit your area in the near future. Most of the clinics are free and open to the public, but some require preregistration.*

☐ *Sign up for a one- or two-day Leave No Trace course. There is also a five-day master class, but you have to be 18 to sign up for that one.*

☐ *Leave No Trace also offers a free online course if you want to get a brief overview.*

☐ *Don't forget to check out the LNT scholarships that are available.*

chapter 8

Grown-up Children and Grandparents

Growing up in Nashville, I didn't realize how lucky I was. I took the trails for granted. Within about 3 miles of our house were two city parks and one state park that had 75 miles of hiking and horseback trails. I grew up playing ball sports, so I didn't make much time for backpacking or camping until I got to college, but when I came home I started going on hikes and trail runs every chance I got. Neither of my parents could join me on the runs. My mom had had multiple knee surgeries. As for my dad, the only running he did was to the grocery store for a gallon of milk.

When my sister and I came home from college—or from our *peregrinations* abroad, as my grandmother would say—we'd usually fly off in different directions, spending time with high school friends we hadn't seen in months or visiting our favorite burrito joint for a cheap meal. But it also became an unwritten rule that on a daily basis, two, three, or all four of us Davises would head to Radnor Lake for a hike on the Lake Trail, the South Cove Loop, or Ganier Ridge.

I don't want to over-sentimentalize it, but something special happened on those hikes. We had some of our most meaningful conversations as a family on them. And when my sister and I were living in another state or a foreign country, to walk on that soil—the soil of middle Tennessee—reminded us of where we came from and of our culture, our family, and our roots. It grounded us.

So much about Nashville has changed in the last twenty years—high-rise condos have filled the Gulch, trendy restaurants have popped up where honky-tonk dive bars used to be. And the traffic keeps getting busier. Our family keeps changing too. My parents are getting slower, Charley's getting more adventuresome, and we keep increasing our numbers.

Teton Valley, Jackson, Wyoming
MP (MEGAN PETERSON) PHOTOGRAPHY

About the only thing that doesn't change is the trails. Someday when my parents are gone, my family will visit Nashville, and while we're there we'll go for a walk on that familiar ground. We'll do it because it brings back good memories. We'll do it because it's what we've always done. We'll do it because it's good medicine.

—Brew Davis

SEASONS OF LIFE

They say that when you have young children, the days last forever and the years go by in the blink of an eye. One day you're wiping their bottoms; the next you're dropping them off at college. A few years after that, you're moving them into their first apartment; and before you know it, you're holding your first grandchild.

Fortunately for all of us, hiking is a lifelong hobby. In fact, one of Jen's favorite sayings is this: "The trail is there for everyone at every phase of life." Sure, life speeds up for your children as they grow, but there's no reason you can't hit the trails with them when they reach college and adulthood, particularly if you started hiking together when they were young and they want to keep the tradition alive.

The period when your children are young adults can actually be a real golden age for hiking. You may still worry about them a little when you're on the trail together, but you won't have to microManage them anymore. They are able to pack for themselves, do their own camp chores, and route-find with confidence. The roles may even start to reverse; your kids might be the ones taking things out of *your* pack to lighten the load or lending *you* a hand as you rock hop across a stream.

Trails in every corner of the world offer seemingly endless possibilities. And whether you take a short hike from a rental cabin in Colorado, spend the day exploring the Andes, or trek hut-to-hut across the Alps, you and your kids are at the perfect age to maximize adventure and appreciate the experience. The trail is there to help you grow together as you grow *up* together.

"The trail is there for everyone at every phase of life . . . to help you grow together as you grow *up* together."

Hiking is a lifelong hobby
that can span generations.
©THINKSTOCK.COM/MONKEY
BUSINESSIMAGES

The College Years

When your child is in college, you'll have plenty of competition for quality time. Chances are your son is not at home anymore, and when he does come home he is busy visiting old high school friends and haunts—and you are left struggling to schedule much QT. So if you really want to have a meaningful conversation with your son or catch up on everything that he's been up to, consider scheduling some time for a hike. If he's resistant, suggest the hike as your Christmas, birthday, Mother's Day, or Father's Day gift. He'll be grateful he doesn't have to run to the outlet mall at the last minute. And it'll keep another unwanted necktie or bottle of cheap perfume out of your house.

The trail creates space and time for conversation. You don't have to share your son with friends or a cell phone, and it may be a welcome break for him from the paper that's due next week or the stress of his part-time job. And you'd be surprised how much the words start flowing when the hike begins.

If your son or daughter is *really* into hiking, this is a great time of life to start a hiking challenge together. For instance, if you live in the Northeast, commit to section hiking Vermont's Long Trail together. Out west, hike a set number of "fourteeners" in Colorado. Perhaps you want to hike in all fifty states together

Trail Tech

Unplugging and Reentry

Hiking is a great opportunity to disconnect from the rest of the world. Of course the rest of the world doesn't stop when you go hiking. Your inbox is likely to be flooded when you return. Here are a few simple tips to make your reentry less painful and more efficient:

1. Set up an automatic out-of-office message in your absence. Electronically announcing your absence lets folks know that it may be a few days before they hear back from you. Leave a similar message on your work and cell phones.

2. Organize your inbox as soon as you return. Categorize e-mails based on how urgent they are-—one for "urgent" correspondences to be handled within 48 hours, another for "immediate" tasks to be handled within a week, and a third for the e-mails you can take your time with. Sort your mail and prioritize your house chores in the same way.

3. Schedule regular payments. Before you hit the trail, use online banking features to schedule any payments or transfers that need to occur while you're out of pocket.

or cover every trail in a particular national park. (For example, the Smokies have more than 800 miles. Talk about a summer project!) Even if you're not interested in peak bagging or covering an extended area, establishing a hiking challenge gives you something to work on together over an extended period of time. For urban areas, try simply getting out of the metropolitan area for more challenging paths.

As difficult as it can be when your child leaves the nest, it can be even more difficult to accept that he now wants to hike alone or with his peers. In the first place, you feel rejected. And on top of that, he may put himself in harm's way. But it's important to remember that this is a season where he's wanting and *needing* to spread his wings. There will be other opportunities for you to hike together in the years ahead, but right now it's good for him to branch out on his own. Hiking by himself or with his buddies is a great opportunity for him to come into his own as a hiker and a person, and those are things he can't fully do when he's on the trail with you. Besides, experiencing the trail apart also gives your child the opportunity to miss you, and to appreciate all those wonderful, selfless tasks you performed on overnight backpacking trips. Sometimes you need to spend a few miles apart to realize what a great hiking partner you have. As for potential hazards, if you've trained him well in those formative years, he should be on the right course. If not, encourage him to bulk up on his backcountry knowledge by taking trips with his college outdoor club.

In the meantime, remember your family unit is not confined to your children. Maybe your father wants to spend quality time with you, or perhaps a cousin, niece, or aunt wants to take a hike. If the urge and the void are still there, look into volunteering with a local Scout club, trail group, or mentorship organization that gets children on the trail.

Take the opportunities to hike with your son or daughter when they present themselves. Even if the family hiking opportunities seem a little lean during these years, you can still set a positive example and leave an outdoor legacy for your child to follow by giving of your time and exposing others in your community to the trail.

"Your family unit is not confined to your children."

Fifty Is the New Forty

If you or your significant other has reached middle age, you're probably wondering something like "Where did the time go?" or "How did I get so old?" or "Where did I put my car keys?" The definition of "middle age" is always changing, but generally it seems to be anywhere from 40 to 65. That said, there are plenty of people in this age range who act anything *but* middle aged. Jen's mother, for example, remained in the young adult class at her church until she turned 60! (To her credit, she did look very young—and she still does.)

Plenty of other middle-age individuals consider themselves to be too old for the youthful adventures they once entertained. But no matter your years, age is just a number, and being middle aged might be one of the best times in your life to be a hiker. It is, after all, like a fine wine or an expensive European cheese; some things just get better with age.

A good time for all— young or old
LORI PARSELLS

By the time you hit your mid-40s, your children are self-sufficient, allowing you more time to enjoy the trail. This is a great time to rediscover your significant other—you know, that person you pass in the hallway during midnight feedings or in the driveway on your way to and from your teen's soccer or play practice. After surviving the first couple decades of parenthood, it's nice to remember both who you are as an individual and who you are as a couple. And if you're a single parent, you may finally have time for that trail club or meet-up group you've been meaning to join. If you've started dating someone, the trail is a great place to get to know each other. Hiking dates mean no dressing up for dinner or wondering who pays the bill. On the trail, conversation is your entertainment and the distractions are good ones—spotting wildlife or taking in a spectacular view (romantic picnic, anyone?).

In this season of life, many people look for new or inventive exercise routines. As your metabolism slows, it could be time for you to incorporate more cardiovascular workouts to stave off those extra pounds while keeping your blood pressure low and your quad and calf muscles strong.

In fact, hiking might be the answer to some of your health needs:

- It's cheaper than a gym membership.
- The scenery's always changing.
- You can make it as difficult or easy as you want it to be.

If it's been a while since you've hiked, you might notice that your muscles and joints are a wee bit more sore than when you were a twentysomething backpacking across Europe. If you've never used hiking poles before, consider investing in a pair to help reduce the impact on knees, hips, and ankles, especially if your hikes take you on a lot of uphills and downhills. Reduce your pack weight to relieve the stress on your body—but don't do this by removing essential items. Instead shop for lightweight or even ultralight gear that will cut back on your load without sacrificing comfort or safety.

If you have hiking dreams that you want to accomplish, make a list so you can prioritize the more challenging, technical ones while you're still in good health. And push those less difficult hikes toward the bottom. After all, you'll need something to work on in your 70s and 80s.

The Golden Girls (and Boys)

We've met hundreds of senior hikers over the years who are active members of their local trail clubs. They are some of the best trail maintainers and most ardent trekkers we know. They spend several days a month maintaining trails and several days a *week* on half- and full-day hikes. As younger adults, we're

Trail Mix

This trail mix features an adult drink. Hot beverages are a great pick-me-up on a cold day or a nice way to end an overnight backpacking trip. As important as it is to enjoy alcohol responsibly off the trail, it's just as important to drink in moderation on the trail. It's a no brainer that you don't want to drink and drive, but you really shouldn't drink and hike, either. Have you ever tried to interpret a map or navigate a confusing trail network while intoxicated? Neither have we—and we never want to. Besides, any form of alcohol—whether denatured for your stove or distilled for your belly—adds pack weight. And don't let your senses deceive you: Alcohol is not an effective method for staying warm on a cold night. It might offer temporary relief, but studies have shown that consuming alcohol can inhibit your ability to assess your body temperature. So it can cause a lot more harm than good. Just a little food for thought—er, drink for thought.

A Backpacker's Hot Toddy

5 ounces water

1 lemon tea bag

Honey

2 ounces whiskey

Bring 5 ounces of water to boil. Add lemon tea bag and let steep. Mix a spoonful of honey and stir until dissolved. (Most grocery stores have individual honey sticks or packets that are lightweight and portable, but you can also squeeze it straight from the plastic bear.) Add 2 ounces of whiskey, give it another stir, and enjoy.

©ISTOCK.COM/DGERRIEPHOTOGRAPHY

real story

The Meaning of Family

There is a peacefulness in the wilderness that is hard to find anywhere else. Every hike I go on leaves me in awe and wonder; I know I have my parents to thank for this reaction. When I think about what my family means to me and what I've learned from my parents, my mind immediately goes to backpacking. My oldest and fondest memories of my family are associated with hiking, camping, and backpacking. When I was little, we car camped regularly throughout California—Point Reyes, Stanislaus National Forest, Yosemite.

When I was 14, my parents took my brother and me on our first backpacking trip: a four-day foray into the Yosemite backcountry. As an angsty teenager, I was not in the physical or mental shape to take on a 30-pound pack and hike 5 to 7 miles a day. My dad will tell you I complained incessantly and maybe even cried a little. At 23, I can no longer imagine a fulfilling life without hiking, backpacking, and being outdoors.

By taking their daughter on that first backpacking trip, my parents planted the seed that instilled in me a deep-seated love of nature. We've now been on countless camping and backpacking trips, hiking up to 20 miles a day and staying out in the backcountry for nine days. It's crucially important to me that we get to do more before my parents can no longer go.

Hiking hasn't just built my character; it has also allowed my family to truly become an unbreakable team. From carrying the food and the shelter, to finding the trail, to making dinner, to singing to keep our spirits up, we've created memories, jokes, and bonds that will last a lifetime. On our last backpacking trip, we were caught in a thunderstorm that brought pouring rain and pea-size hail to our low-lying campsite. Together we dug trenches around the tent, made sure our bags stayed dry, and funneled the water out of our camp. The storm passed, and soaking wet and covered in mud, we spent the rest of the night joking about our professional level trench-digging skills.

I can't thank my parents enough for taking my brother and me on these trips, and I hope to instill these same family values and love of nature in my future children. Now, as a young adult, I can't wait for the times I get to spend outdoors with my family. To the parents of young kids or teenagers who may not want to go outside or walk for miles, I can only encourage you to persevere despite their complaints. Start with short hikes, take them to see waterfalls and big trees, bring or make delicious snacks, and involve them in the process of reading maps and planning trips. I promise they'll end up loving it.

—Ella Clarke

often humbled by the skill, energy, and enthusiasm of our older trail friends. Numerous hikers in their 60s and 70s have completed long-distance trails in the United States. Lee Barry walked the entire Appalachian Trail when he was 81. Dozens of retirees travel around the globe to explore trails in different countries. And we know countless others in our very own Carolina Mountain Club who have climbed forty or more 6,000-foot peaks in the Southern Appalachians or who have hiked to all twenty-four fire towers in the western part of the state.

Some senior hikers are more hard core than others. Jen's grandfather, for example, kept a very brisk pace and rarely stopped for anything when Jen joined him for a walk (no wonder she became an endurance hiker). Some grandparents join their kids and grandkids for a hike only to get antsy when their 5-year-old granddaughter has to stop for one potty break after another. Others don't want to go too hard, too far, or too fast. But regardless of whether senior adults hike with purpose or sit in peace and solitude, they're generally filled with a gratitude for trails and for wilderness that other demographics can learn from. There are a number of similarities between the way a young person and an old person interact with the wilderness. Adulthood fills us with distractions and interruptions, and it takes either the beginning or the end of life to truly appreciate nature.

*Tongue River Valley,
Wyoming*
DAVIS FAMILY

When you become an older adult (or if you've already become one), we hope you hike. Hike however you see fit, wherever you see fit. Set a challenge and rediscover the competence and confidence of your youth, or take it easy and just enjoy taking it all in. If you are a not a senior adult but you have older relatives, make it a priority to take *them* on the trail with you. You not only learn ways to positively interact with nature through observing their trail habits, but you also have the opportunity to learn from their stories. Senior adults have a lifetime of experience and wisdom. On the trail they have time to share these life lessons with you, and they can be not just a hiking partner but also a life coach.

If you're a senior adult and you didn't pick up lighter gear and hiking poles in your 50s, it is a good idea to look into them now because they can prolong your hiking career. Some senior hikers get so comfortable with hiking poles on the trail that they continue to use them off-trail for balance as they age.

Be aware of some health-related things that most younger hikers don't have to worry about, especially joint pain and osteoporosis. The rate of hip- and knee-replacement surgery is much higher for this demographic; if you or someone you know experiences increased pain or soreness in these regions, cut back on your trail routine until you've had a chance to meet with an orthopedic specialist. And if you've already undergone orthopedic surgery, incorporate stretches into your pre- and post-hike routine. You may even consider yoga, which has the ability to improve recovery time and agility on the trail for older hikers.

You may not move with the same speed as when you were younger or climb the same peak, but hiking still yields positive health benefits. For one thing, it puts less stress on your joints than running does, and it requires less lateral movement than sports like tennis or squash. Even if you can't hit singletrack like you used to, walking on greenways or packed gravel roads can lower blood pressure, prevent the onset of disease, and delay premature aging. And there are just as many emotional, mental, and spiritual benefits to moving through a natural setting as there are physical. No matter your age, you're never too old to go for a hike.

next step

Hiking is the original outdoor activity, but it gives you a great baseline of fitness for participating in other recreational sports. Hiking can be, quite literally, the first step in a multisport adventure. That's because many of the most amazing spots for paddling, skiing, and climbing across the country must be accessed by foot. So the next time you take a hike, look for ways to expand your love for trails into other outdoor pursuits. You'll probably find that the added perspective—not to mention the cross-training—will increase your love for walking, as well. Here are some ideas, for starters:

- ☐ **Mountain biking.** *Some downhill mountain bikers hike their bikes up steep mountains so they can come careening back down on two wheels.*
- ☐ **Paddling.** *You may have to portage kayaks, rafts, or canoes across land to reach the river or the next rapid. On paddling trips in places like Minnesota's Boundary Waters, there can be portages of up to a mile with your boat and gear.*
- ☐ **Backcountry skiing.** *Some of the best backcountry spots require a hike up to the starting location, complete with skis secured to your back as you go.*

chapter 9

Health Conditions and Special Concerns

I once had the privilege of working at a camp for adults and children with special needs. We hiked together on a regular basis, and my campers were terrific guides. Often I'd pass by a tree or rock without giving it a second thought only to have my camper stop and marvel at its shape, color, and texture. My companions noticed the noises and smells more than I did, and I'll never forget their joy at seeing the most commonplace woodland creatures. A mischievous squirrel was always cause for laughter; it was worth the wait to stop for a turkey vulture circling in the distance; and spotting a turtle along the path was like finding a priceless treasure. On these hikes, distance never mattered. My campers didn't care if we walked 2 miles or 200 yards, so long as they spent time in this magical place.

The trail is there for everyone at every phase of life. That encompasses individuals with special considerations. We have been fortunate to hike with quite a few deaf or blind people, one of whom hiked tens of thousands of miles over the most rugged terrain in North America with only his guide dog for sight. We've listened with intrigue as parents described taking children with cystic fibrosis and cerebral palsy into the woods on a routine basis. We've met hikers who have dealt with restrictions like diabetes, eating disorders, and hypoglycemia, and we've become cyber friends with others who have covered incredible distances with prosthetic legs.

Every day people overcome obstacles to hike. My own closest experience came when I backpacked extensively during my second and third trimesters of pregnancy, and it was successful for three reasons. First, I followed in the footsteps of other hikers who had experienced a similar journey. I knew it could be done because I'd seen it done before. When Brew and I were thinking about being parents, we crossed paths with a woman backpacking the

Sandy beaches in the High Sierras
ELLA CLARKE

Colorado Trail in her second trimester. And she looked so healthy and happy. Hiking while pregnant was modeled for me, and that gave me the confidence to do it too.

Second, we talked to my doctor before backpacking. I had a very supportive and well-informed doctor who gave me some simple lab tests so she could monitor my health and hormone levels while I was hiking. We discussed the risks and the benefits. After talking it over in depth with her, I felt safer and more confident about our journey—both on the trail and through pregnancy.

And third, hiking felt good to me, comforting even. While pregnant, I had trouble sleeping and my hormone levels made me feel like a stranger in my own body. Running hurt, I wasn't allowed to play contact sports, my diet was limited, and alcoholic beverages were out. Even relaxing in a hot tub was out. And yet . . . I could still hike. Not far and not fast. But I could get out in nature and feel empowered. And when I hiked, I actually felt like myself.

The personal satisfaction I derived from hiking during a challenging time in my life is a universal experience. The trail is therapy. We have met individuals on the trail recovering from major surgery or an accident, suffering with PTSD, an emotional disorder, or experiencing great loss. And all of them say the same thing: There's something cathartic about getting out in nature and putting one foot in front of the other.

We've heard it said, "There are no such things as problems in this life, only opportunities." Well, the trail is a perfect place for each of us to embrace those opportunities.

—*Jennifer Pharr Davis*

A PEP TALK

We want to encourage families who have specific needs and considerations to get on the trail. Unfortunately, there's not enough room in this book to address every specific difference. And we're not here to sugarcoat the challenges, because they will be many. Mistakes will be made, meltdowns will be had (by your children and you), failures will take place, and limitations will be realized. But that's not the end of the story. The point is that you got out there.

Kellisa Cain, an amazing young woman who has cerebral palsy, is one such person who got out there. Kellisa may never hike the entire Appalachian Trail, and she may never climb Mount Everest. But thousands of people have done both of those things, and to our knowledge, no one else has ever hiked in all fifty states quite like Kellisa. If they have, they certainly haven't done it with as much style. For more on Kellisa, check out her Real Story later in this chapter. In Jen's first memoir, *Becoming Odyssa*, she mentions that her

Do a search for trails that have the specific access you need.
©THINKSTOCK.COM/
DANIEL_KAY

Appalachian Trail hike helped her become the best version of herself. That's what life's all about, isn't it? Not comparing yourself to anyone else, but rather comparing yourself to your *best* self and figuring out how to achieve that.

Now, with that pep talk under our belts, let's get down to the nitty-gritty, shall we?

GETTING STARTED

Proper research and planning is always important, no matter who's hiking. But it's especially important for families who have special considerations. *Before doing anything else*, seek the counsel of your doctor. Make a list of questions to discuss, and tell him or her what you're hoping to do. Once you're on the same page with your health care provider, seek the wisdom of a parent or family who has hiked in similar circumstances. Perhaps this person has done the trail you're about to do. Or maybe she just has a wealth of knowledge about backpacking. Either way, she'll see some angles you don't and help you anticipate pitfalls. In the end, this conversation should be empowering and allow you to avoid the mistakes others have made while also re-creating their successes. If you don't know anyone with hiking experience, track down a trail organization in your area for insight. Search online for blogs by families who have a child with Down syndrome, for example. You can glean loads of information and inspiration from these reports. Reach out to outing clubs in your area for kids with ADHD or autism. Or, if you prefer, mainstream your child in a day camp or club for kids without differences. There's a plethora of resources out there, so don't feel as though you have to dive in without knowing how deep the water is.

And just like any other family who is hiking for the first time, remember to take it slow. One thing we remember from driver's education class several decades ago is that for every unusual circumstance, you need to increase the distance between you and the car in front of you by 1 second. If a normal following distance on the interstate is 3 seconds but you're driving at night and it's raining, bump that up to 5 seconds. If you're behind an enormous semi-truck, push it up to 6. Similarly, if you're hiking uphill with three kids, you won't be able to go nearly as far as if you're hiking with one kid on a flat, smooth greenway. If one of them is a toddler who refuses to be carried, take that into account. If another is autistic, that should factor in too. You can always increase your pace and miles, but focus on getting comfortable on the trail before setting bigger goals.

Pregnancy

So what *should* you expect when you're hiking while pregnant? The short answer? Anything. Sometimes you'll feel so lethargic that you'll think you can barely lift one foot in front of the other. Other times you'll have that other-worldly pregnancy strength that allows you to grow another human *inside* of you while juggling everything else in your life. And that strength also helps you reach the top of the mountain.

When you start to show, make sure your pack's hip belt fits comfortably around your waist. A proper pack is designed to put the weight on your hips, but

Jen, six months pregnant with Charley, finishing a 500-mile trail through the Spanish Pyrenees
DAVIS FAMILY

if the belt digs into your abdomen, it'll be really uncomfortable, and you'll need to either adjust it or find a better-fitting pack. It's also very important for expectant women to eat and drink frequently on the trail, even on more urban pathways with flatter surfaces. Your typical snack and hydration routine ain't gonna cut it. Step it up a notch—remember, you're eating, drinking, and hiking for two.

Hiking can be very difficult in the first trimester due to nausea and fatigue. If you don't feel this way, don't rub it in! For everyone else, the good news is that a hike—even a short one—can energize you, allow you to sleep better at night, and even improve your focus. Doctors often prescribe light therapy for women dealing with prenatal depression, and what better way to get light therapy than to spend time on a trail?

The second trimester is your golden window for hiking. At this point, you're not carrying *too* much extra weight, and *most* of the time you'll feel better and have more energy than you did the first trimester. So take advantage of it. Consult your doctor, but typically it's safe for a woman in this stage of pregnancy to backpack and enjoy fairly challenging day hikes. But do avoid strenuous, technical trails where the risk of falling is greater.

The third trimester will see you trudging—if not crawling—toward that dreaded/blissful finish line the OBGYNs call a "due date." Although it's harder to hike now because of the *person* inside of you, it's still one of the best things you can do for your sanity and for the physical health of you and your baby. Hiking during the third trimester can ward off additional baby weight. You might think, "Does it really matter at this point? I'm already a whale." To that we have three responses. First, stop it. You look gorgeous. Don't let anyone tell you otherwise. Second, keeping your weight down in the third trimester helps you bounce back much quicker after delivery. Third, think of how much easier hiking will feel after you've gotten that little bowling ball out of you.

Programming Note

Before we get into this next section and the sections that follow, let's reiterate something: You know your children much better than we ever will. *You know what they love and hate, what gets them going, and what sets them off. We'll do our best to share what we know and think while treading lightly on this subject and the ones that follow. Just know that when it comes to your children and your family, you are the expert. And more than anyone else, you are best suited for guiding them down the trail both literally and metaphorically.*

Twinsies, Trios, Quartets, Etc.

We are *so* impressed by parents who hike with multiples. It's hard enough playing man-to-man defense on the trail with a newborn, but playing zone can be downright impossible. In those early years, you may want to recruit a close friend or relative to help you. Another option is to join a local hiking club. Chances are there are a handful of senior adults who are more than happy to help you because they're missing their kids and grandkids who live on the other side of the country.

When your children start to toddle, it's possible to get away with having one walk by your side while the other rides in a carrier. But monkey see, monkey do—so when one's walking the other will probably want to walk too. That's okay so long as you plan wisely (e.g., not going for a hike when you need to pick up your kindergartner in half an hour).

By the time they enter elementary school, you should be able to hike the same way a family does with children of varying ages.

Asthma

Asthma can be aggravated in the backcountry just as it can in the frontcountry. But it can also be controlled with proper care and medication, so it shouldn't prevent you from hiking. In fact, research shows that exercise and time spent outdoors can reduce stress for asthma sufferers, which in turn prevents asthma attacks.

Don't worry—you're not seeing double.
BRYAN SHAEFFER

If your son has a daily prescription, make sure he's diligent about taking it leading up to and during a hike. Individuals who have experienced asthma often have accoutrements, like a peak flow meter, a fast-acting bronchodilator (usually an albuterol inhaler), or even a nebulizer at home. Definitely bring your equipment on the trail with you, no matter how much pack weight it adds. If you don't already have one, you may also want to invest in a battery-powered nebulizer. And just as you would inform a soccer or swim coach about your child's condition and how to help him manage it, you'll want to do the same with any adult or mature teen who's hiking with you.

Factors that are especially important to adults and children with asthma include seasonal allergies, air quality, extreme weather, and extreme exercise. If you know that ragweed affects your child's condition, avoid hiking in the early fall. If pollen is an irritant, consider hiking after a heavy rain has washed it away. Air quality can also impact asthmatic hikers. You may already be familiar with the local air quality website airnow.gov, but you'll need to pay special attention to this if you're going into the backcountry. You won't have to worry about pollutants as much, but other irritants can be worse in the wilderness than in urban and suburban settings. Generally speaking, "moderate" and "good" conditions are typically safe for hiking, but once the rating decreases to "USG" ("unsafe for sensitive groups"), you should probably postpone your hike until a later date.

With regard to extreme temperatures and extreme exercise, stick with easy or intermediate hikes in moderate weather conditions until you have a sense of what your child is comfortable with. *Note:* There's a lot of debate in the medical community about the use of epinephrine to stave off asthma attacks. We're in no position to tell you what to do here, but if you have asthma or carry an EpiPen and are curious about what to do in case of a first-time attack, educate yourself on the opposing sides.

There's also the potential for a child or adult to experience asthma for the very first time while on the trail, since the same factors that can affect a preexisting condition (anaerobic activity, seasonal allergies, extreme weather, and anxiety) can also bring on a first-time attack. And once an attack sets in, there's not a whole lot that can be done. The best thing you can do to prevent an attack is to make sure no one's overexerting him- or herself.

But let's say your daughter does start to struggle with breathing. You'll need to decide whether she can be evacuated and whether you need to call 911; then you should consider moving her if you think your location might be causing the reaction (e.g., away from a grove of trees or a patch of wildflowers where the pollen count is high). If the reaction doesn't seem too severe, see if a few minutes of rest bring her back to an equilibrium. Fear and nerves can make things worse, so be as Zen as possible, and remind everyone else in the group to do the same. Once she's able to regulate her breathing, cut the hike short and schedule a visit with your doctor when you get home.

If the wheezing or labored breathing continues, or if she's too weak to be evacuated safely, then sit her down, look her in eyes, and encourage her to follow your breathing pattern as you inhale through your nose and exhale through your mouth with pursed lips. It can also help to count the time that passes as you do this (for example, "Inhale, two, three, four . . . exhale, two, three, four . . ."). Continue to breathe together and reassure her until help arrives or you can evacuate. If you have a caffeinated drink on hand, it's worth giving her a sip or two, since caffeine can relax airways and reduce the lungs' response to irritants. Just don't give too much, because that can cause her heart rate to rise.

Asthma attacks are terrifying but, as with all other matters of first aid, preparing thoughtfully can eliminate many of the variables that trigger them. If you do your homework, think through possible scenarios, and pack the right equipment, you should be in for a delightfully uneventful trail experience.

Autism Spectrum Disorder

Jen once led a four-day retreat for a group of high school students, one of whom was diagnosed with high-functioning autism. On their first day he said, "I don't like hiking, but I do like views and animals." To which Jen replied, "I think we can work with that." Each day the group covered 4 to 8 miles over moderate terrain before heading back to the lodge. The autistic student was never forced to hike the full distance, but he always chose to, even though it took him up to an hour longer than his classmates. By the end of day four, he was keeping up with the group and was extremely proud of what he'd accomplished that week. He even admitted that although the views and animals were still his favorite part, he'd started to like the hiking too—just a little bit.

Time spent in nature can decrease sensitivity among individuals with ASD.
©THINKSTOCK.COM/
MARIADUBOVA

A 2010 presentation at the International Symposium on Society and Resource Management said time spent in nature can decrease sensitivity among individuals with Autism Spectrum Disorder (ASD) while also improving their communication, emotional expression, cognition, interaction with others, and physical fitness. We all know there are benefits that come from connecting children with nature, but parents of children with autism know that it can be difficult to anticipate which specific parts of nature their kids will connect with and which will be detrimental. For some children with autism, the sound of a crashing waterfall might be too much; others might find it mesmerizing. Some might revel in the sound of the birds or the wind in the trees, while others might be frightened by those unfamiliar sounds. As for actually hiking, your child might find it tedious and mundane. Or he might fall in love with the rhythm and repetition. After all, in a world that can be overstimulating for all of us, there can be something very comforting about simply putting one foot in front of the other.

"**Fear and nerves can make [asthma] worse, so be as Zen as possible . . .**"

We know a New England family who takes their autistic daughter hiking every day. We were able to join them one afternoon and were fairly certain their daughter would have kept hiking as long as they let her. The parents stick to their daily hikes because they believe their daughter benefits from the routine, and they see a marked improvement in her demeanor on the days they hike. As an added benefit, the exercise helps her combat the potential weight gain that's a side effect of her medication.

The steps we recommended earlier in this book for acclimating your children to the outdoors (e.g., starting in your own backyard and exploring city parks before heading to a remote trail) can be especially helpful for children with ASD. There's always the chance you could head straight to the wilderness and have your child connect immediately, but because new environments can be overwhelming, you'll likely have more success by introducing them to the outdoors in small doses, even starting at a city park or on a short bike trail. Talk through what you might see and hear on the trail, showing videos and photos of animals and plants to prepare your child for the newness of it all. One of our favorite blogs from a family with a child who's autistic is hikeblog love.com. It's no longer active, but it contains archives with loads of helpful information as well as inspiring photos.

Stop to smell the flowers.
DAVIS FAMILY

Attention Deficit Hyperactivity Disorder (ADHD)

Like most of these special considerations, attention deficit hyperactivity disorder has an array of symptoms, and its severity can vary greatly. Diagnoses have risen sharply over the past two decades. So has the amount of research out there, and much of it has documented the positive effects of green space for kids with ADHD.

Frances Kuo and Andrea Faber Taylor, two professors at the University of Illinois at Urbana–Champaign, have studied the effects of nature on kids with ADHD for the past eighteen years, and their research suggests that these kids display increased attention spans after spending time in a natural setting. Taking it a step further, they've also found that the greener the environment, the more dramatic the effects.

Some children with ADHD might be reluctant to go for a hike or spend time in nature if it's not part of their upbringing or culture, but studies show that being outdoors is healthy for kids with ADHD, regardless of their background. Taylor and Kuo also found that spending time in nature is effective for children with ADHD regardless of gender, ethnicity, and socioeconomic background. And a separate study released by the professors in 2011 proposed that time spent in green space can actually reduce the symptoms of ADHD over time.

If you're child has ADHD and you're convinced that getting her in a natural setting is a good thing but you're not quite sure how to do it, the good news is that you don't have to go far. The research suggests that even urban green spaces like city parks with an abundance of trees, flowers, boulders, and other natural features can yield great benefits. Arboretums or botanical gardens also prove beneficial, since they tend to be even more fecund than the average city park.

Children with ADHD respond well to both structured and imaginative playtime in outdoor settings. Consider letting your child with ADHD roam free for half the outdoor time and then switching to a game or activity for the other half. It is helpful to take plenty of breaks so that she has opportunities to interact with nature rather than just pass by it. If she's really getting into something, let her sink deeper into it, whether that's taking time to photograph a spiderweb, getting down on her hands and knees to smell a flower, or taking her shoes off to soak her feet in a cold mountain stream. (For more on this subject, check out *Outside* magazine's article "ADHD Is Fuel for Adventure": outsideonline.com/2048391/adhd-fuel-adventure.)

Amputations and Paralysis

If you've been paralyzed or had an amputation during the course of your life, you obviously won't approach hiking in quite the same way as a hiker who has full use of his limbs. That said, you can still experience every type of trail imaginable. In fact, we know of a number of people dealing with these issues who have gotten into hiking *because of* their amputation or paralysis, not in spite of them. And those hikers have made a habit of doing some pretty remarkable things.

For example, in 2004 Scott Rogers hiked the entire Appalachian Trail with an above-the-knee amputation. And despite the fact that she is paralyzed from the waist down, an Ohio woman named Stacey Kozel began an A.T. thru-hike in 2016 on custom electronic leg braces. A California man named Bob Coomber (aka, "4WheelBob") has gotten his wheelchair to places most people would never

©ISTOCK.COM/MARTINBOWRA

imagine, including to the top of 14,000-foot mountains. And the gist of this entire book may best be summarized in a beautiful, 5-minute tearjerker of a video that tells the story of Bob Headings, a paraplegic who went to the bottom of the Grand Canyon with the help of his sons and grandsons. (Here's the link: youtube.com/watch?v=v4UiFMlacxg. Just makes sure you have a box of tissues handy.)

A couple of factors determine how quickly and to what degree you can hit the trails after an amputation or paralysis. The first is your fitness level. If you're a sporty type with a low resting heart rate and a toned physique, your muscle memory and experience as an athlete should make the transition easier than if you are starting from scratch. Factor in the length of time between your injury and/or surgery. Wait until the swelling goes down, the scar tissue has healed, and you've recovered the necessary muscle mass to support forward, backward, and lateral movement before doing anything too intense.

If you're in a wheelchair, buy a pair of full-fingered neoprene or Kevlar gloves. A court chair with good-traction tires is fine on greenways and dirt and gravel roads, but the wide wheelbase makes it difficult to navigate over

It's amazing how much healing power nature has.
MP (MEGAN PETERSON) PHOTOGRAPHY

singletrack. If you really get into hiking and can afford it, consider a carbon-fiber or titanium chair. That said, trail chairs are too long, wide, and heavy for some people. 4WheelBob, for example, uses a clone of his everyday chair, with shock absorbers, multilinked suspension in the rear, and custom bracing to account for the lack of a foot plate. He also recommends learning to wheelie through mud and water, canting the rear wheels at 0 degrees, and avoiding aggressive, knobby all-terrain tires because they can tear gloves to shreds in a matter of miles.

Amputees have a lot of decisions to make too—whether to get a vacuum, pin-lock, or air-suction prosthetic; whether to buy a silicone, polyurethane, or other liner; the material and thickness of your sleeve, etc. As with a new pair of boots, any wheelchair or prosthetic

needs to be broken in. Before heading to the trail, make sure you or your family member tests the equipment thoroughly on short hikes over flat, smooth surfaces. If you're an amputee, you may also want to try hiking with one or two poles for increased stability.

Whether you have a wheelchair or prosthetic, you'll probably experience some level of discomfort until you get things dialed in. Ointments can lubricate at the point of contact. There are dozens to choose from—Vaseline, Bag Balm, Two Toms, coconut oil, etc. You may find the perfect one right away or you may discover that none of them really do the trick. (Brew has been dealing with chaf-ing for over a decade and he still hasn't found a foolproof solution.) Keep tinker-ing but also know that an ointment may not be enough; you might have to make an adjustment to your hardware. You can always go back to the doctor or pros-thetist if the fit or ride is uncomfortable. Consider the distance of your hike and what it might do to you physically. Most Appalachian Trail thru-hikers, for exam-ple, lose a lot of weight, which can affect their prosthetics. When this happened

to Niki Rellon, who became the first female amputee to complete an A.T. thru-hike in 2015, she had to find someone to alter her prosthetic mid-hike because her knee was chafing so badly.

You may also face backcountry-specific challenges. For example, if you've had an arm or hand amputated, it may be difficult to filter water or put up a tent. But there are creative ways around these issues (e.g., treating your water with iodine tablets and finding a tent that uses only poles with elastic to make assembling them easier), and these challenges are probably no different from those you've faced in everyday life, whether driving a car, helping your daughter dress, or baking a cake. The good news is that trails and medical technology are improving and becoming more accommodating.

Call your local parks and rec department or trail organization to ask about adaptive or wheelchair-friendly paths in your area. A group of amputees or paraplegics may have a meet-up near you for hikes and other outdoor adventures. One such group is Denver-based Paradox Sports (paradoxsports.org), which leads trips and climbing workshops around the country.

You can also research rails to trails (R2Ts) routes (railstotrails.org). Rails to trails are fairly popular. As the name suggests, these trails have been converted from defunct railroad routes. They're typically wider, and whereas hiking paths can have grades up to 30 or 40 percent, R2Ts rarely get out of the single digits. They're also usually covered in asphalt or packed dirt, so they're appropriate for most wheelchairs, though occasionally you'll find sand or wood chip sections.

Besides doing basic recon on distance and elevation change, it's also a good idea to find out as much as you can about the tread (what the trail is made of), water crossings, and the trail's overall difficulty. If possible, scout the route before making a full day trip of it. Once you find a specially outfitted wheelchair and develop a strong upper body, you'll be ready to take on lengthy uphill R2T inclines and more rugged terrain. The sky's the limit. Just ask 4WheelBob.

Blind and/or Deaf

Almost all the people we know with vision and hearing impairment face life's challenges head on, and the trail is no different for them. By navigating the uneven terrain of our nation's footpaths, they embody the old adage "Where there is a will, there is a way." And that goes not just for shorter, urban hikes but also long trails. One blind-deaf hiker named Roger Poulin completed the Appalachian Trail in 2014; his SSP (service support provider) Roni Lepore, who hiked the entire way with him, was deaf. And our friend and fellow North Carolinian Trevor Thomas (trail name "Zero/Zero") has hiked more than 20,000 long-distance miles all over the country with his dog, Tennile.

Then again, Rome wasn't built in a day. And the A.T. wasn't hiked in a day. So if you're looking to get into hiking and you or a loved one has hearing or vision loss, start in a familiar setting and on nontechnical terrain. A local greenway, for example, is a good place to practice new techniques before heading to more remote, challenging paths. Resources that are commonly used in town, such as a white cane or service animal, are also useful on the trail, and techniques often used in foot races, such as lead ropes or harnesses, prove effective on the right terrain.

Hiking poles are especially beneficial for blind or vision-impaired hikers, as they help with both landscape definition and balance. But we should add a word of caution here: If you tend to trip a lot and you're hiking over uneven terrain, you might not want to use the pole's wrist straps—it can sometimes be difficult to free your hands from them and brace yourself for a fall. If you have a service animal that you want to take hiking with you, incorporate hiking into its training, starting with longer walks close to home, and consider looking into additional classes or private instruction to prepare you and your animal for the trail.

Take some precautions with hiking hazards that are at least partially detected through sound. For example, if you plan to travel through an area with increased wildlife, attach bear bells to your pack, travel in a group, or sing occasionally. If an animal hears someone coming, it usually will avoid a sighting and confrontation.

If you're hiking with a deaf and blind hiker, occasionally ask him what he picks up with his other senses, since the ones they have use of are usually much stronger than those of people with a full range of sight or sound. We've been told that deaf hikers can sense thunderstorms, waterfalls, and other bodies of water through vibrations and changes in the atmosphere. Blind and/ or deaf hikers can identify nearby campsites, towns, and animals before their sighted companions because of their stronger sense of smell. And, assuming they didn't eat Doritos for lunch, they're often first to notice the taste of the trail—sweetness after a spring rain; a dry, chalky taste in the hot summer; or earthiness in autumn as fallen leaves decompose on the ground.

Cystic Fibrosis (CF)

After Jen became pregnant with Charley, we learned that she had the cystic fibrosis gene. Brew also got tested, and his results came back negative. Still, a few weeks later at an ultrasound, a specialist told us there were some indicators that our baby had CF.

We told her that was impossible since I wasn't a carrier and she matter-of-factly told us they only test for the most common strands and that there were hundreds of rare varieties that don't show up. Before we had a chance to

This trail in Pittsburgh has terrific views and is accessible for all kinds of hikers.
DAVIS FAMILY

process what she'd said and ask follow-up questions, she promptly concluded the appointment and left the room.

Beyond being frustrated by the doctor's abysmal bedside manner, our prevailing concern was that we had *no idea* how to care for a child with CF, so we went home and researched it immediately. As people who love to hike, one of our first questions was "If our child has CF, will we be able to get outdoors?"

To our relief, we found ample research to the affirmative, as well as plenty of firsthand accounts from families whose children have cystic fibrosis. In fact, studies suggest that engaging in moderate exercise can suppress the symptoms of CF and can improve the overall quality of life for those affected. Further research uncovered articles and tips from renowned hospitals and medical groups offering advice for children and adults with CF who want to start exercising. For example, the Cystic Fibrosis Foundation offers a downloadable PDF (cff.org/Living-with-CF/Treatments-and-Therapies/Fitness/Day-to-Day-Exercise-and-CF) with information and suggestions for starting

an exercise routine—hiking being one of the recommended cardiovascular exercises.

If you or your child is affected by CF but isn't yet active, your doctor may perform an exercise test to determine lung capacity and a baseline fitness level. From this, he or she can recommend specific activities, appropriate lengths of time, and intensity levels. A person with cystic fibrosis dealing with a respiratory infection or heart condition might be asked to avoid exercise or monitor her levels more closely.

When hiking on a trail, extreme heat and humidity can have an increased impact on individuals with cystic fibrosis, so try to hike during the cooler seasons of the year. If you have a strong penchant for hiking in the summer months, get out early or late when the heat index isn't so high. Since those with cystic fibrosis lose more salt than the average person when they sweat, pack plenty of fluids. Bring along a sports drink and salt or electrolyte replacement tablets to combat the loss of sodium. Or make your own electrolyte drink mix, which allows you to raise the sodium content as needed.

Digestion and caloric intake can also be an issue; pack lots of energy-packed goodies for the trail, not to mention pancreatic enzymes to absorb the nutrients. Most hiker foods like trail mix, PB&J, cheese and crackers, summer sausage, and fresh fruit already fall into this category.

It turned out Charley didn't have CF, but since Jen is a carrier we still feel connected to the cystic fibrosis community and are always happy to meet kids with CF on the trail. We'll never forget a hike in Vermont several years ago where we met two girls with CF. Their parents got them out almost every day and were convinced that was one of the best things they could do together as a family.

If you don't have cystic fibrosis but love hiking and want to support the community and ongoing research, consider signing up for an Xtreme Hike to raise funds and awareness. You can learn more about these challenges, which are held all over the country, at fightcf.cff.org.

Cerebral Palsy (CP)

The effects of cerebral palsy are wide-ranging. Some individuals with CP have an unsteady gait, while others can't walk. Some have trouble gripping things, while others have full use of their hands. And some can speak and communicate clearly, while others have limited speech. But the effects of exercise for people with motor impairment are just as wide ranging. According to the National Center on Health, Physical Activity, and Disability, it can include all of the following: increased participation in individual and community activities; improved sense of well-being and a reduction in anxiety; increased lung and heart efficiency; increased strength, flexibility, mobility, and coordination; improved bone health; weight control; and a reduction of chronic diseases and secondary conditions.

Regardless of the ways cerebral palsy affects you or your family, you can and should get outside to enjoy the trails on a regular basis. Going for a hike stimulates cognitive function for individuals with cerebral palsy; it also improves communication skills and increases motor skills. Some folks with CP use technology to assist them with daily functions and communication. And while these tools are amazing, it can be healthy for kids with CP to take a respite from their screens and electronic devices every now and again.

Because cerebral palsy impacts balance and body mechanics, some hikers with CP like to use poles to steady themselves. But others might have trouble gripping objects, so for them the hiking poles could be more of a burden than a benefit. The different gait and uncontrolled movements that hikers affected with cerebral palsy can have means they expend quite a bit more energy than hikers without CP. Because of that it's a good idea to keep initial outings short until hikers can build up endurance.

real story

Families on Foot—and Wheels

After many hours of research, I found the perfect first trail to share with my 5-year-old daughter, Kellisa. I loaded the minivan with everything we would need for the 430-mile drive. I selected the 0.3-mile West Ridge Falls Access Trail in Amicalola Falls State Park for one reason: It was wheelchair accessible.

I doubt many people would drive close to a thousand miles round-trip for a trail that is so short and easy. However, at the time I didn't think we had any other options for my daughter, who has cerebral palsy. The trail led to a beautiful view of Amicalola Falls. I should have been thrilled to have my daughter out in such a wild place for the first time, but I couldn't help but feel disappointed that the hike lasted less than 10 minutes.

Chris Kain and his daughter, Kellisa, at Cleetwood Cove, Crater Lake National Park
LISA MARIE KAIN

From the accessible trail, I could see another viewpoint far below us. We drove around the park until I found the trailhead to the platform I'd observed from above. I was excited to learn that this was the Appalachian Approach Trail. It was obvious to everyone (except me) that we had no business starting up this trail. The hike was steep, wet, and muddy. In short, it was not blazed with wheelchairs in mind. Kellisa was in her therapeutic chair designed for level, hard surfaces. I struggled with my first steps, and she cheered me on with her giggles. A few people suggested that we turn around because there was no way we could make it up the trail, and a few other hikers offered to help. But I was determined to get Kellisa to the top under my own power. As I gasped for air, we reached the platform.

At Black Mesa
MATT BUCKINGHAM

Before Kellisa was born, I had hiked to the top of a couple of 14,000-foot mountains, but nothing compared to this accomplishment. As they say in mountaineering, getting to the top is only half the adventure. I still had to get Kellisa safely down this trail. I said a few prayers as we slipped and slid our way down to the bottom, with Kellisa giggling the whole time. I prayed, "If we get down without Kellisa getting hurt, I promise we will never do anything like this again." As soon as we got back to the minivan, I looked with pride at Kellisa's excited face and muddy wheelchair.

Then a lightbulb went on in my head. A whole set of possibilities started racing through my brain as it became obvious that I wasn't going to keep my promise in that prayer. Since that day in May 2004, Kellisa has hiked all across the United States on trails developed for feet, not wheels. Since that first hike, we've moved beyond wheelchairs and now use specially adapted mobility devices. Kellisa has had many firsts for a disabled girl—The Narrows, Cleetwood Cove, Black Mesa, and Grand Island, to name just a few. It's all worth it; I strongly believe that Kellisa feels normal when out on a trail blazing our own path.

—Chris Kain

There's no limit to the length that hikers with CP have gone. A man named Wesley Tremble hiked the entire Pacific Crest Trail with cerebral palsy. His gait wasn't as rhythmic as other hikers, but he still hiked 2,650 miles from Mexico to Canada, traversing through deserts and 13,000-foot mountains in just four and a half months. (This video chronicles his adventure: vimeo.com/109846546. You can also visit Wesley's website, wesleytrimble.com, to read about his other adventures and see that Wesley credits his parents with instilling a love of nature in him. In fact, his parents hiked a 14,000-foot mountain with him when he was just 10 months old!)

Another avid hiker with more severe cerebral palsy symptoms is Kellisa Kain. Kellisa was born fifteen weeks premature and weighed only 2 pounds, 1 ounce. She was diagnosed at a young age with cerebral palsy and epilepsy. But her father, Chris, vowed to help her live the fullest life possible.

Kellisa is now a teenager who loves to travel, hike, and camp. As Chris said, "Kellisa has been pushed to many places wheelchairs weren't meant to

go—20 miles across a desert in one day, mountain summits, canyon bottoms, through swamps, and many other places as we travel across North America." Father and daughter have hiked in all fifty states together, but instead of walking with two feet they call their mode of transportation "pushiking." Chris usually pushes Kellisa in a wheelchair, though he has also done things like pull her on a raft through The Narrows in Zion National Park. (If you want to learn more about Kellisa's story and about pushiking, you can visit her website: www.kellisaspath.com.)

We mentioned earlier that spending time on the trail can increase cognitive function and communication skills, and Kellisa is a prime example of this. Chris said she had been unwilling to speak new words even though she could have done so. But on a particular day hike in Oklahoma, Kellisa had a breakthrough and, as her dad describes it, spoke more new words in that one hike than she had in six months of speech therapy. The trail helps people to become the best version of themselves, and that certainly seems to be happening for Kellisa and Chris.

©ISTOCK.COM/JFOLTYN

Diabetes

On her very first night backpacking, Jen camped next to a guy who had type 1 diabetes. She'd already been anxious about performing all her camp chores and spending the night in the forest for the first time when the guy beside her in the shelter said, "Hey, if I don't wake up in the morning, can you look in my pack and give me some glucose?"

Can you imagine? Your first night backpacking and the guy next to you isn't sure he's going to wake up in the morning?! Jen readily admits that the fellow was much better prepared than she was. He'd been out on the trail for several days without a hint of trouble monitoring and controlling his blood sugar levels and was just mentioning his condition as an extra safety precaution which, incidentally, is *always* a good idea. The point of this story, though, is that the stakes for hikers with diabetes can be quite high.

And managing insulin levels can be very different on a day hike versus an overnight backpacking trip. Obviously, backpacking is an extended form of exercise and involves carrying a heftier load, so persons with diabetes (PWDs) need to account for that and may need to monitor more frequently and consume more carbohydrates than on a shorter outing. Test your management routine on several day hikes before heading out for a multiday excursion. If you're taking a longer trip, ask your doctor if sensors and a pump are a more effective way to handle your insulin levels.

Just as the amount of food and water you bring depends on the duration of your hike, so does the amount of insulin and other medications. Whatever the trail length, pack more than enough of everything, including syringes, insulin pens, a pump, prescription meds, glucose, etc. Those extra couple pounds mean nothing compared to the predicament you'll be in if you run out of something because you cut it too close when packing for the trip (side benefit—you'll get stronger than all your nondiabetic friends).

If you don't already have a backpack, consider buying one with large pockets on the hip belts and sides so you can access snacks and medicine without completely taking it off. If you need more space or if you've back-packed for a while and like your current pack, add a waist pack. If you wear an insulin pump, find a pack whose hip belt doesn't interfere with where your pump is located. You may be able to customize it or get an experienced friend to help you work around your pump location.

It can be tricky to keep insulin at the right temperature, but it's certainly not impossible. Carry it and other meds in an insulated container. Or keep the meds in the interior of your pack where they're insulated by your clothing, sleeping bag, and other gear. If you're worried about extreme heat, fill a bottle with springwater and tuck it in next to your meds. Or buy small, light "frio packs" online, which you can wet and rewet to keep meds cold. Test out cold and warm weather hiking on day hikes first so that you'll have a better game plan for overnights. If you're still having trouble, you might need to avoid camping in extreme temperatures altogether.

Another consideration, particularly on the East Coast and in the Pacific Northwest, is moisture. On an extended backpacking trip, ambient moisture can affect test strips, so make sure you keep them in a waterproof container. Doubling up on ziplock bags is a cheap, lightweight alternative and works just as well as anything else.

Many PWDs hike by themselves but it's a good idea to hike with someone who can administer insulin or glucose if necessary. When you hike in a group, ideally one or more people could monitor glucose levels and provide insulin in an emergency situation. If you don't already have one, you should wear proper identification on the trail—such as a medical ID bracelet—or at least carry medical-alert identification (e.g., driver's license) in your pack. We also recommend buying a Glucagon kit, which is an emergency medical device used to treat severe hypoglycemia if you pass out. It's sort of like an EpiPen for PWDs.

Whatever quick and easy snacks you pack with you on the road should translate pretty well to the trail. Meals may be a little tougher to plan out since a lot of hiker dinners involve noodles, dehydrated mashed potatoes, and refined cereal products. Then again, that stuff isn't the most healthy or appetizing for anyone, so you may enjoy tracking down healthier options and more interesting recipes. Low blood sugar on the trail can be a big danger so we suggest bringing more food than you think you need. It's also very important to stay hydrated so that your body can properly process food and glucose. Even on a day hike it's a good idea to pack a water filter or iodine tablets and to have a good sense of water source locations before you hit the trail.

Hiking with diabetes can seem complicated at first. But once you get your packing list squared away and your on-trail insulin levels figured out, you should be in for some great adventures.

Down Syndrome (DS)

One memorable trail experiences Jen had at her camp job was a hike with a 40-year-old woman with Down syndrome (DS). The woman didn't mind the hiking, but what she really enjoyed were the snack breaks. On this particular hike they had a snack every half-mile or so, and before long they ran out of food. Normally that wouldn't be an issue on a 2-mile hike, but when the woman realized the food was gone, she staged a "sit-down strike" on the trail.

Despite being nonverbal, she was a very strong communicator. Whenever Jen encouraged her to stand up and start moving, she shook her head and wagged her finger. There was no way Jen could have carried her the final mile, and she never found a way to motivate the woman. Eventually Jen just sat

The trail is there for everyone, regardless of ability.
©THINKSTOCK.COM/ND3000

down beside her hiking companion and kept her company for most of the afternoon. Finally, at dinnertime, the woman decided she was ready to go back. While she was eating, someone stopped by and asked her if she had enjoyed the hike. Ever silent yet expressive, the woman nodded emphatically, flashed a toothy grin, and gave Jen an enormous hug. The next day she held a 4-hour sit-in at the pool because she didn't want to leave.

Getting people with Down syndrome on the trail has loads of benefits for them, but a number of physical factors need to be taken into consideration. People with DS tend to have weaker lung capacity and lower maximum heart rates, as well as less muscle tone, higher rates of obesity, and—because of increased flexibility—are more likely to dislocate joints—especially hips—on outings. Like the rest of us, they also tend to shut down whenever they get pushed beyond their limits. But their limits are less extreme, and they can be very strong willed. The upshot of all this is that, if you're getting your child or young adult with DS on the trail for the first time, take it easy on those first few trips.

Since people with DS sometimes have less refined motor skills, as well as poor depth perception and balance, hiking poles can be useful. And as Jen found out, having some sort of reward system can be useful too. But as with other low-impact forms of exercise, like jogging, dance, yoga, and water aerobics, the benefits of hiking for people with DS can be tremendous. In short, it can offset all the issues listed above (strengthen their heart rate, increase lung capacity, improve muscle tone, and push them beyond the brink of what they thought possible). And exercising in a natural setting might be just what the doctor ordered for individuals who haven't yet found the right physical outlet.

Two adventurers who did just that are Appalachian Trail hiker "Tutu" and Everest Base Camp climber Eli Reimer. In 2013 Tutu (so named because she wore a frilly pink skirt) hiked over 1,000 miles of the A.T. with her mom, sister, and brother. Farther afield, Eli Reimer trekked 70 miles through high-altitude conditions with his father to reach the 17,600-foot camp in Nepal. By doing so, Eli raised more than $85,000 to help families of kids with Down syndrome and other conditions.

Mental and Emotional Health Concerns

Hiking happens to be one of the most accessible and affordable forms of therapy around, whether you've had a rotten day at work or are dealing with a mental health condition. For centuries, mental health and wellness centers have incorporated wilderness therapy into their recovery regimens. In the 1800s, doctors prescribed "camp cures" for urbanites dealing with mental and emotional imbalances. The belief was that cities took something out of a person that nature could put back into them—and modern research has only reinforced this notion. Wherever you live, there's probably a teen program near you that's helping young people overcome addiction, behavioral issues, low self-esteem, and mental health concerns. There are similar programs for adults across the country, as well as programs like Warrior Hike (part of Warrior Expeditions: warriorexpeditions.org) that afford servicemen and women the opportunity to "walk off the war."

In her talks, Jen often says, "The trail gives you what you need." And that's certainly true for people facing emotional disorders, addictions, post-traumatic stress disorder (PTSD), and for those suffering the loss of a loved one. Hiking offers space and time to process events, clear your head, and reflect on who you are and what you want to be. It presents a clear challenge on which to focus. It wears you out, which can reduce nervous energy and allow you to sleep more soundly at night. It removes outside distractions and gives people the opportunity to stay on the straight and narrow—both literally and figuratively. Even when a person feels tangled or stuck, simply taking a step—and then another, and another—up and down mountains, through valleys, and across wilderness can be incredibly cathartic. Jen often says, "The trail is a metaphor for life." And there's just something very powerful about positive, continuous forward motion.

chapter 10

Where to Go

Even before we became parents, we knew that spending time in nature and getting on hiking trails would be part of our family culture and identity. But we never dreamed of hiking in all fifty states with Charley by the time she was 2 years old. Our original goal was to hike in as many states as possible over the course of a summer during one of Jen's speaking tours. It quickly morphed into an eighteen-month adventure—with a child.

For eighteen months we crisscrossed the country, watching Charley grow from an infant to a crawler to a toddler. And all of it was in the context of the trail. She spent her first Father's Day watching me finish a trail race at a state park in Ohio, and she took her first steps on a riverside trail in Des Moines. She saw her first black bear on the Mountains-to-Sea Trail in Asheville, her first gator on a boardwalk near New Orleans, and her first moose on a hike in Denali. Even her first words sprang from the trail. She learned to say, "Be gentle," when touching columbines in Colorado and "No cactus!" to remind herself not to get pricked in the California desert. Everywhere we went we found trails, learned new things, and created memories together. It was gluttonous, really. The sort of thing most people never get to do. Or else they do it after retiring from forty years on the job. Our good fortune is not lost on us; we still look back on that time in wonder.

We are committed to getting families outside because we have witnessed the benefits of the trail firsthand. Throughout our travels and the network of friends we've met along the way, we discovered family-friendly trails that we knew had to be shared.

We rarely arrived in a new town with a firm idea of where we'd hike. Our schedule and our daughter dictated otherwise. Instead, we'd ask the locals

Blue Ridge Parkway trail
©THINKSTOCK.COM/SDBOWER

about their favorite spots. And we were never disappointed. No matter what our expectations were of a place, we always found something worth exploring.

We've also had the good fortune of hiking abroad on several occasions, and we hope we can keep doing it. But our biggest takeaway from eighteen months on the road was that we could spend the *rest of our lives* exploring the United States and we'd only scratch the surface. This is a beautiful country, friends—from the granite coasts of Maine to the black sand beaches of Hawaii, from the swamps of Florida to the glaciers of Alaska. It's all just waiting to be explored.

We leave you with a quote from the greatest advocate for wilderness our country has ever known, John Muir:

Walk away quietly in any direction and taste the freedom of the mountaineer. Camp out among the grasses and gentians of glacial meadows, in craggy garden nooks full of nature's darlings. Climb the mountains and get their good tidings. Nature's peace will flow into you as sunshine flows into trees. The winds will blow their own freshness into you and the storms their energy, while cares will drop off like autumn leaves. As age comes on, one source of enjoyment after another is closed, but nature's sources never fail.

Online Resources

There are dozens of websites devoted to connecting hikers with trails. Here are the half dozen or so we've found to be the most useful and user-friendly:

KRISTOFFER ISRAEL

alltrails.com: This site pulls up a map and lists all the options in your area. Search by home-town or specific trail, park, or nature preserve.

backpacker.com/trips/states: Look up hikes by state or zip code on this sub-page of *Backpacker* magazine, which is a great resource for hikers. Oh, and you can get a free subscription when you become a member of American Hiking Society (americanhiking.org).

fs.fed.us: The USDA Forest Service site has a fun and interactive visitor map. Once you find a national forest near you, you can pull up information about specific trails, including GPS coordinates, driving directions, and what you'll find at different trailheads.

nps.gov/index.htm: The National Park Service website helps you plan your visit by offering things to do, including day hike and backpacking options.

rootsrated.com: This site has an interactive map of the United States and lists outdoor "experiences" of every sort (wind surfing, disc golf, road running, etc.). Trail-centric experiences include hiking, trail running, backpacking, and camping.

trails.com: Trails.com has a database of popular trails in different cities, states, and national parks. It also has a directory for Canada, a forum, and a page called "Outdoors 101" with articles on everything from rain gear and boot maintenance to choosing the right hiking poles.

Long-Distance Trails Aren't Just for Hiking Long Distances

The United States has dozens of long-distance trails. And while we certainly don't expect you to walk out the door tomorrow to tackle one of these behe-moths, they pass within hours or even minutes of *hundreds* of towns and cities across the country, and they provide day hikes and overnight outings for every ability and experience level.

Below are the websites and a brief overview for the longest national scenic trails. (We've included the others in the state listings.) We hope you'll consider becoming a member of these associations or making a donation to support them and the national treasures they protect.

The Appalachian Trail, Pacific Crest Trail, and Continental Divide Trail make up the "Triple Crown" of American long-distance hiking. If you were to compare thru-hiking to higher education, the AT would be like a bachelor's degree, the PCT like a master's, and the CDT like a PhD, with the degrees of difficulty (no pun intended) based on how often you can resupply, how easy or hard it is to find the route, and how many people attempt a thru-hike each year.

appalachiantrail.org: The 2,189-mile Appalachian Trail is the longest hiking-only footpath in the world and passes through fourteen states along the East Coast.

continentaldividetrail.org: The Continental Divide Trail is 3,100 miles long and crosses New Mexico, Colorado, Wyoming, Idaho, and Montana. It's sort of a "choose your own adventure" with different routes depending on the time of year and what the weather is doing at higher elevations.

northcountrytrail.org: Another trail worth mentioning here because of its sheer length is the North Country Trail. The NCT stretches *4,600 miles* across New York, Pennsylvania, Ohio, Michigan, Wisconsin, Minnesota, and North Dakota. It's very difficult to complete in a calendar year because of its length and the longer winters up north. There aren't a lot of thru-hikers on it, but it's growing in popularity with day-trippers and weekenders.

pcta.org: The Pacific Crest Trail runs 2,650 miles along the West Coast and travels through California, Oregon, and Washington. Cheryl Strayed's best-selling book *Wild* brought national attention to the PCT in recent years.

Hiking State by State

Below is a list of the trails we hiked as well as trail clubs listed state by state, plus the District of Columbia. Entries with the AHS boot print are the trails we've hiked. We also included a number of long-distance trails that we hope to complete someday. This should only be a starting point. We suggest you reach out to your nearest outfitter or trail organization to learn as much as you can about the local scene.

Who knows? Maybe someday you'll have your own fifty-state adventure and be able to check all or some of these hikes off your list while making a new list of your own.

The Davis family—Jennifer, Charley, and Brew—enjoys a break from the trail.
DAVIS FAMILY

1. Alabama

Trail: White and Blue Trails
Park: Oak Mountain State Park
City: Pelham, Alabama (near Birmingham)
Description: Oak Mountain is a terrific state park with beautiful waterfalls, hardwood forests, and some serious climbing. For the most part, we stayed on the ridge and connected the White and Blue Trails to make a loop. Peavine Falls is supposed to be impressive after a hard rain, and there are plenty of the other amenities you'd expect to find in a state park.
More information: alapark.com/oak-mountain-state-park-hiking-trails

Long-distance trail: Pinhoti National Recreation Trail
Park: Talladega National Forest
Description: The Pinhoti Trail is a 335-mile long-distance trail that runs from Talladega National Forest in east Alabama to Springer Mountain in north Georgia (which happens to be the starting point for those heading north on the Appalachian Trail). Part of the Great Eastern and Eastern Continental Trails, there's a 100-mile ultramarathon held on it every November for masochists. The trail blaze is a turkey foot, which is fun and also very fitting for Alabama.
More information: pinhotitrailalliance.org

2. Alaska

Trail: Rock Creek Trail
Park: Denali National Park and Preserve
City: Denali Park, Alaska
Description: We hiked this 2.4-mile trail near the park entrance on our first day in Denali. It travels from the visitor center through the taiga to park headquarters

real story

Hiking Goals

I challenged my family to hike in all of the Indiana state parks in 2010. My wife, Bonnie, and I have always loved visiting state parks. As a matter of fact, we were married at Spring Mill State Park in Mitchell, Indiana. Hoping to instill a love of the outdoors in our children, we set out to experience all that the state parks had to offer.

We have always looked for ways to spend family time in the outdoors, and I thought this to be an obtainable goal. The stipulation was that we would hike no less than 2 miles in each of the state parks. My wife and my three girls (Morgan, 15; Megan, 13; and Madison, 7) accepted the challenge, although the girls were not as excited as my wife and I. We planned for three months, equipping ourselves with some good hiking shoes, backpacks to carry supplies, moleskin, sunscreen, bug repellent, and plenty of water and snacks.

We started our adventure on April 2 at McCormick's Creek State Park—Indiana's first state park. For fun on the hikes, one of the games we played was seeing who could spot a grand-daddy longlegs first. Although they may have thought it was silly at first, the Micklers are very competitive. We enjoyed park after park, most being day trips from our home; however, we took a week's vacation to visit the nine northernmost state parks. We battled the elements, some bugs, and one big snake on the trails, but we also grew closer together as a family and shared lots of laughs and good times. We hiked in temperatures as high as 93°F, and on December 9 we finished up our last hike in 33°F and snow.

Happy to accomplish our goal for the year, we had a celebration dinner. When I asked our daughters what goal we could set for the next year, our oldest daughter said we should visit all of Indiana's Dairy Queens! We feel so blessed for the time we spent together that year in the great outdoors. Happy Hiking!

—Larry "Turtle" Mickler, avid hiker, husband, and father of three

©ISTOCK.COM/HAMACLE

and the sled dog kennels. (If you book in advance, you can catch a sled dog demonstration.) We made a loop with the Roadside Trail, but you can also catch a shuttle back to your car if you're tired. **More information:** nps.gov/dena/plan yourvisit/rock.htm

 Trail: John Hunter Memorial Trail (formerly Solomon Gulch Trail)
Park: Chugach National Forest
City: Valdez, Alaska
Description: We read somewhere that this 3.8-mile hike is one of Bear Grylls's favorites, probably because the trailhead is just past the Solomon Gulch Fish Hatchery, where he can scarf down all the dead salmon that are floating in the bay. (Don't worry; you climb uphill very quickly and leave the smell behind.) The climb to Solomon Lake is all uphill, but much of it follows a gravel road, so it's actually pretty moderate. Views of the lake and of Valdez from above the power

If the mountain goat can make it to the summit, so can we!
DAVIS FAMILY

station are worth the effort. Another interesting hike near Valdez is the short one up to the Exit Glacier, which is receding faster than Jason Statham's hairline.
More information: valdezalaska.org/place/john-hunter-memorial-trail

 Trail: Middle Earth
Park: Kincaid Park
City: Anchorage, Alaska
Description: Our friend Sue from Anchorage took us to Kincaid Park on one of our last days in Alaska. For a city park, it blew us away. It has miles of trails, loads of coastline (with rocks that are just perfect for skipping), and incredible views across Cook Inlet. Bonus: The trail we hiked on was called Middle Earth, so Brew got to pretend we were hiking toward Mordor.
More information: muni.org/departments/parks/pages/parkdistrictsw.aspx

Long-distance trail: Resurrection Pass
Park: Chugach National Forest
City: Hope, Alaska
Description: We're dying to get back to Alaska to hike this 39-mile gem on the Kenai Peninsula. It's rife with 360-degree views, spring wildflowers (for, like, the last week of June—all the "spring" Alaskans get), and wildlife like moose, Dall sheep, and mountain goats.
More information: www.fs.usda.gov/recarea/chugach/recarea/?recid=13398

3. Arizona

 Trail: Echo Canyon Trail
Park: Camelback Mountain, Echo Canyon Recreation Area
City: Phoenix, Arizona
Description: While we were in Phoenix, we climbed the 1.3-mile Echo Canyon

A pair of cairns and a pair of cliffs in Sedona, Arizona
DAVIS FAMILY

Trail to the summit of Camelback Mountain. It did have some steep drop-offs, so if you're squeamish about heights, you might want to take the Cholla Trail instead. Both are strenuous and shouldn't be attempted in the heat of the day, but if you're in shape and can hike early (or late) enough, the views from the top will make you forget the climb.
More information: phoenix.gov/parks/trails/locations/camelback-mountain/trails

Trail: Bear Mountain Trail
Park: Coconino National Forest
City: Sedona, Arizona
Description: We hiked several trails in Sedona, and you really can't go wrong here. The area is as gorgeous as they say it is. But our favorite was the 5-mile out-and-back up Bear Mountain. There were great views the entire time, and Charley saw her first rattlesnakes ever on the way up. Don't worry; she was in her kid pack.

And she may have actually been asleep when we saw the second one.
More information: www.fs.usda.gov/recarea/coconino/recarea/?recid=55222

State trail: Arizona National Scenic Trail
Description: The AZT is another bucket list hike for us. It's 800 miles and stretches from Mexico to Utah, winding through the Sonoran Desert, the Grand Canyon, and miles of wilderness in between. As the Arizona Trail Alliance website proclaims, "It is the backbone of Arizona."
More information: aztrail.org

4. Arkansas

Trail: East Summit Trail
Park: Pinnacle Mountain State Park
City: Little Rock, Arkansas
Description: If you and your family like to channel your inner mountain goat, have we got a trail for you! This

steep 1.5-mile out-and-back will lead you through a sizable boulder field to a summit with spectacular views of the Arkansas River Valley. Just be prepared to use your hands and take your time. For a more gradual descent, take the West Summit Trail and complete the 2.5-mile loop back around to your car.
More information: arkansasstateparks .com/pinnaclemountain

Long-distance trail: Ouachita National Recreation Trail
Description: The Ouachita Trail travels 223 miles through the Ouachita National Forest from central Arkansas to eastern Oklahoma. We got to hike around the trail's eastern terminus in Pinnacle Mountain State Park, and it definitely made us want to hike the rest of it.
More information: friendsot.org

Sometimes there's no telling where a trail will lead you.
DAVIS FAMILY

Long-distance trail: Ozark Highlands Trail
Description: Arkansas actually has two scenic trails. In our opinion, the Ozarks are one of the most underrated regions in the country, and if the 218-mile OHT looks anything like what we saw around Fayetteville, it must be a pretty sweet walk.
More information: ozarkhighlandstrail .com

5. California

Trail: Rock Pool Trail
Park: Malibu Creek State Park
City: Calabasas, California
Description: Who knew that Malibu had hiking trails? We sure didn't until we visited this state park where they used to film scenes for the TV show *M.A.S.H.* It's amazing how quickly you can escape the hubbub of the city, even in a city as big as L.A. And it's not hard to do in this beautifully quiet setting. There are 15 miles of trails in the park. We chose the Rock Pool Trail along Malibu Creek because we needed the shade on a hot summer day.
More information: www.parks.ca.gov/ ?page_id=614

Trail: Crissy Field Promenade
Park: Golden Gate National Recreation Area
City: San Francisco, California
Description: Jen had an event at an outdoor store near here and we had a little time to kill, so we walked along the Crissy Field Promenade, which has beautiful views of Alcatraz, the bay, and the Golden Gate Bridge. We've done a lot of other hikes in California. Heck, Jen hiked the entire length of California on the Pacific Crest Trail and climbed to the

top of Mount Whitney while she was at it. But these hikes just go to show that you don't have to "escape the city" to escape the city, if you know what we mean.

More information: nps.gov/goga/index .htm

Long-distance trail: John Muir Trail
Description: The JMT runs 215 miles from Yosemite National Park to 14,596-foot Mount Whitney, the tallest mountain in the lower forty-eight states. So yeah, it's a pretty sweet hike. It runs mostly along the same route as the PCT but is obviously much shorter, so it's the perfect foray into long-distance hiking for West Coasters.
More information: pcta.org/ discover-the-trail/john-muir-trail

6. Colorado

Trail: Bear Creek Trail
Park: Bear Creek Preserve
City: Telluride, Colorado
Description: We did this 4.5-mile out-and-back to scenic Bear Creek Falls because it's wide and smooth. Also, the elevation gain is minimal compared to other local trails, so it can be a good choice if you're not yet acclimated to hiking 8,750 feet above sea level. We've been to Telluride a bunch and have done a lot of hiking around there. Other notables are the Jud Wiebe Memorial Trail, Bridal Veil Falls, Silver Lake, Valley Floor (a flatter option), and the 17-mile trail to Ouray via Imogene Pass. (This one's not so flat. Be sure to shuttle a car around unless you want to climb back over the mountain on some really tired legs.)
More information: visittelluride.com/ activity/bear-creek-trail

A late fall hug in the Tetons
MP (MEGAN PETERSON) PHOTOGRAPHY

Trail: Bluebell-Baird Trail
Park: Chautauqua Park
City: Boulder, Colorado
Description: It seems kind of funny to include a trail for Boulder given that everyone we know who lives there is hard core into outdoor sports. But maybe there are some Boulderites out there who haven't gotten into hiking yet—or folks who are planning a visit and wondering where to go. Chautauqua Park is the entryway into Boulder's beloved

Flatirons. We just stuck to the Bluebell-Baird Trail because it was short and sweet, but the park is chock-full of trails and is the perfect place for an evening hike or trail run after work.
More information: bouldercolorado.gov/parks-rec/chautauqua-park

Trail: Green Mountain Trail
Park: William Frederick Hayden Park on Green Mountain
City: Lakewood, Colorado
Description: This is another great spot for a hike or run after work. It's a short drive from Denver, it gains a lot of elevation quickly, and you're rewarded for all that hard work with spectacular views of the Front Range and the distant Denver skyline.
More information: lakewood.org/HaydenPark

Long-distance trail: Colorado Trail
Description: The Colorado Trail was the first long-distance trail we ever hiked together, so it will always be a special trail for us. It runs almost 500 miles from the San Juan Mountains outside Durango to Waterton Canyon near Denver and mostly follows the Continental Divide. The Colorado Trail Foundation calls it "mile for mile the most beautiful trail in America," and it's hard to argue with the claim.
More information: coloradotrail.org

7. Connecticut

Trail: Housatonic River Walk
Park: Appalachian National Scenic Trail
City: Kent, Connecticut
Description: This beautiful stretch is a favorite for thru-hikers not only because it's one of the rare flat sections between Georgia and Maine but also because of its scenic beauty. You can start anywhere you like, but we recommend the section south of Bulls Bridge Road.
More information: berkshirehiking.com/hikes/bulls_bridge.html

For more information on hiking in Connecticut, contact the Connecticut Chapter of the Appalachian Mountain Club (www.ct-amc.org/CT/index.shtm).

8. Delaware

Trail: Hidden Pond Trail
Park: Brandywine Creek State Park
City: Wilmington, Delaware
Description: Open fields, forested trails, rock ruins, and a creek crossing—that's a lot of action in a 2.8-mile beginner-friendly hike. And your kids will enjoy the Brandywine Creek Nature Center, which has daily programs on local culture and natural history.
More information: destateparks.com/park/brandywine-creek

For more information on hiking in Delaware and beyond, contact the Wilmington Trail Club (wilmingtontrailclub.org).

Twins! Again!
BRYAN SHAEFFER

9. Florida

Trail: La Chua Trail
Park: Paynes Prairie State Park
City: Micanopy, Florida (near Gainesville)
Description: This 3-mile adventure leads to an observation deck where you can scan the prairie for alligators, birds, and feral pigs.
More information: floridastateparks.org/park-activities/Paynes-Prairie#Hiking-Nature-Trail

Long-distance trail: Florida National Scenic Trail
Description: The 1,300-mile Florida Trail is one of eleven national scenic trails around the country and is very popular with thru-hikers who are looking to do something in winter. Because it passes through the heart of the state from the Everglades in the south to the western end of the Panhandle, Floridians are rarely more than a 90-minute drive from it. The FNST bears witness to the rich cultural history and biodiversity of the state and is maintained by the good people at the Florida Trail Association.
More information: floridatrail.org

10. Georgia

Trail: Springer Mountain
Park: The Appalachian Trail/Chattahoochee National Forest
City: Blue Ridge, Georgia
Description: The 1.8-mile out-and-back from the Springer Mountain parking lot climbs to a bronze plaque that marks the southern terminus of the Appalachian Trail. If you hike Springer in spring, you might catch some thru-hikers beginning their 2,200-mile journey to Maine.

More information: www.fs.usda.gov/recarea/conf/recreation/hiking/recarea/?recid=10539&actid=51

For more information on hiking in Georgia, contact the Georgia Appalachian Trail Club (georgia-atclub.org)

Charley and Brew on a winter hike at Davenport Gap, Great Smoky Mountains National Park
DAVIS FAMILY

11. Hawaii

Trail: Manoa Falls Trails
Park: Honolulu Watershed Forest Reserve
City: Manoa, Hawaii (on Oahu)
Description: Every step of this 1.5-mile round-trip is rewarding—the rainforest surrounding the trailhead is filled with

How ah ya, Hawaii?
DAVIS FAMILY

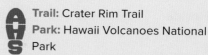

Trail: Crater Rim Trail
Park: Hawaii Volcanoes National Park
City: On Hawaii (the Big Island)
Description: HVNP has 150 miles of trail to choose from, so it can be hard to make up your mind. We got there late in the day and wanted to see the lava glowing at dusk, so we stuck to the Crater Rim Trail. As the name implies, it gave us terrific views of the crater, but it also wandered through lush rain forest at times and was the perfect introductory hike for us. The trail makes an 11-mile loop around the crater, but we chose to do out-and-backs at the observatory and from the Volcano House to Pu'u Pua'i. The Sulphur Banks Trail is also really cool. Actually, it's really hot—scalding hot. So be sure to keep your kids on the boardwalk.
More information: nps.gov/havo/index .htm

12. Idaho

Trail: Tubbs Hills Historical-Nature Trail
Park: Tubbs Hill
City: Coeur d'Alene, Idaho
Description: Tubbs Hill is a park in Coeur d'Alene that's as fun to hike as the city's name is to say. Besides having a number of trails to choose from, there's also access to the lake if you want to picnic, swim, or take an afternoon siesta. We followed the 2-mile Main Trail, which makes a loop and gives you gorgeous views of the lake and town. For a downloadable brochure on the history, geology, and ecology of the region, check out cdaid. org/files/Parks/parks/Tubbs%20Hill/ TubbsBrochuresmaller.pdf
More information: cdaid.org/763/ departments/parks/all-parks/tubbs-hill

bamboo, banyan, and eucalyptus trees, and the waterfall at the turn-around point is gorgeous. Just be sure to stay off those slippery rocks at the base of the falls!
More information: hawaiitrails.org/trail .php?TrailID=OA+19+007

Trail: Waipi'o Valley
City: Honokaa, Hawaii (on Hawaii, the Big Island)
Description: This was our very first stop on the Big Island, and it was worth it. A 3-mile round-trip, it descends a steep, rutted out jeep road for the first 0.75 mile before turning toward the coast and the wonderfully secluded beach. A ride on a rescue chopper here would be spectacular—but really expensive. So don't hike down into the valley unless you're confident you can make it back up. (*Note:* We didn't do this because we had Charley with us, but for a really challenging day hike you can continue on to Waimanu Valley, which is even more secluded than Waipi'o.)
More information: alltrails.com/trail/us/ hawaii/waipio-valley-trail

Long distance trail: Idaho Centennial Trail
Description: The ICT stretches 900 miles from Nevada to the Canadian border. Some of it follows little-used roads, but it offers hundreds of miles of single track as it winds its way through scenic wilderness, stunning mountain ranges like the Sawtooths, Bitterroots, and Selkirks, and rivers like the Salmon and the Snake. Idaho is known as the Gem State, and the ICT is a gem of a trail.

13. Illinois

Trail: Little Grand Canyon Trail
Park: Shawnee National Forest
City: Pomona, Illinois
Description: We had no idea such a dramatic gorge existed in southern Illinois. What a cool spot! The views, birding opportunities, and biodiversity on this 3-mile hike through a box canyon will keep you entertained for hours. And your older kids will have a blast scrambling around rocks and exploring the nooks and crannies at the base of the bluffs.
More information: www.fs.usda.gov/Internet/FSE_DOCUMENTS/stelprdb5404938.pdf

If you want to connect with the hiking community in Chicago, contact the Forest Trails Hiking Club (foresttrailshc.com). In Peoria contact the Pimiteoui Trail Association (ptahike.org).

14. Indiana

Trail: Cowles Bog Trail
Park: Indiana Dunes National Lakeshore
City: Chesterton, Indiana
Description: Don't have the time or money for a summer "vacay" to Florida? Head to Indiana Dunes National Lakeshore instead! We walked the Cowles Bog Trail before heading down to the sandy beaches for a dip and a walk at sunset. There are more than 50 miles of trail in the park, another 16 in Indiana Dunes State Park, which is right next door, and a 9-mile bike trail that runs south from Michigan City. We posted a picture of this beach on Facebook and asked people where they thought we were. They guessed Florida, the Bahamas, and Cancun before saying Indiana. We're not making this up.
More information: nps.gov/indu/planyourvisit/hiking.htm

Trail: Trail #1
Park: Pokagon State Park
City: Angola, Indiana
Description: We visited some friends in Fort Wayne over Labor Day a few years back, and they took us to this terrific state park in the very northeast corner of Indiana. More than a dozen miles of trail crisscross the park and travel

Charley and Brew playing in a creek near Youngstown, Ohio
DAVIS FAMILY

through wetlands, hardwood forests, and along the beaches of Lake James. Pokagon is the perfect place to spend a summer day or weekend, and in the winter there's a toboggan run.
More information: in.gov/dnr/parklake/2973.htm

For information on additional trails in Indiana, contact the Hoosier Hikers Council (hoosierhikerscouncil.org).

15. Iowa

Trail: Fox Run/Legacy Loop/Shea Way
Park: Hitchcock Nature Center
City: Creek, Iowa (north of Council Bluffs)
Description: The 200-foot-tall Loess Hills are remnants of the glaciers that came down into the plains during the last ice age. And the Hitchcock Nature Center just north of Council Bluffs and Omaha is the perfect spot for experiencing them. Ten miles of hiking trails, an observation tower for viewing hawks, and the Loess Hills Lodge visitor center with information on raptors and a "Curiosity Cove" for kids make this a fantastic afternoon activity.
More information: pottcoconservation.com/parks-and-habitat-areas/hitchcock-nature-center

Trail: Hiking Trails and Equestrian Trail
Park: Jester Park
City: Granger, Iowa (northwest of Des Moines)
Description: Jester Park's website says it "has been one of Central Iowa's favorite outdoor playgrounds since 1958." After visiting twice during our book tours, we heartily agree. We walked along the hiking trails and the equestrian trail that runs beside Saylorville Lake and enjoyed watching the blue herons and egrets fishing nearby. Charley loved the playgrounds; there's even an amphitheater with evening concerts in summer.
More information: www.polkcountyiowa.gov/conservation/parks-trails/14-jester-park

Blue herons are good luck, so keep an eye out for them next time you hit the trail.
©ISTOCK.COM/FLOWNAKSALA

Trail: Trout Run Trail
City: Decorah, Iowa
Description: Decorah is home to
Luther College, an annual Nordic
Fest in July, a world-class brewery
(Toppling Goliath), and some of the pretti-
est hiking and biking trails in the Midwest.
We walked along the 11-mile Trout Run
Trail, which had just been completed
in 2012. The paved trail passes bluffs,
bridges, fishing holes, and even a famous
eagle's nest with a momma, papa, and
baby eaglets.
More information: visitdecorah.com/
business/trout-run-trail

16. Kansas

Trail: Nature Trail Loop
Park: Konza Prairie Biological
Station
City: Manhattan, Kansas
Description: Konza Prairie has 7 miles of
hiking trails and was one of Brew's favorite spots on our book tour. He ran the
6-mile loop through lowland forests and
past limestone formations before climbing a ridge with impressive views of the
Flint Hills and the town of Manhattan. It's
right off I-70, so it makes a great stopping
point when you're driving cross-country. If
you're lucky you may even spot the herd
of bison that roams the creek side.
More information: kpbs.konza.k-state
.edu

Trail: Lawrence Mountain Bike Trail
Park: Lawrence Riverfront Park
City: Lawrence, Kansas
Description: Hikers and mountain
bikers share the 9 miles of singletrack at
Lawrence Riverfront Park, so both groups
have to pay attention. But there's plenty
of shade, open prairie, and access to the

*Sometimes the little ones
get plumb tuckered out.*
DAVIS FAMILY

Kansas River. Plus the fairly complex trail
network allows you to make the hike as
long or short as you want.
More information: lawrencemountain
bikeclub.org/lawrence-river-trails

17. Kentucky

Trail: Indian Fort Mountain Trails
Park: Berea College Forest
City: Berea, Kentucky
Description: The trail network at Indian
Fort Mountain provides several options.
A hike to the West Pinnacle or Indian Fort
Lookout reveals beautiful views of Berea
and the surrounding countryside, while
hikes to Buzzard's Roost or East Pinnacle
offer views of the ridges that lead to
Daniel Boone National Forest. You can't
go wrong either way—unless you head
back downhill to the wrong parking lot,
which we almost did.
More information: berea.edu/forestry/
indian-fort-mountain-trail

Jen, her friend Katie, and two tired kiddos in Oak Mountain State Park, Alabama
DAVIS FAMILY

you're driving down I-65, why not stop and take a hike—first aboveground, then below.
More information: nps.gov/maca/index .htm

Long-distance trail: Sheltowee Trace National Recreation Trail
Park: Daniel Boone National Forest
Description: Our hike around Indian Fort Mountain in Berea really intrigued us. The knobs and ridges were like mini versions of our own Blue Ridge Mountains. And the kicker was that we didn't see a soul for hours. So it got us to thinking about the Sheltowee Trace Trail, a 290-mile National Recreation Trail that stretches from Big South Fork National Recreation Area in Tennessee through Daniel Boone National Forest north to Rowan County, Kentucky. Someday we hope to hike it. And here's an interesting tidbit: "Sheltowee" is the name a Shawnee chief gave to pioneer and frontiersman Daniel Boone. It means "Big Turtle."
More information: www.fs.usda.gov/ recarea/dbnf/recarea/?recid=70839

Trail: John James Audubon Trails
Park: John James Audubon
City: Henderson, Kentucky (near Evansville, Indiana)
Description: John James Audubon State Park allows you to travel through peaceful forests and beside still ponds and offers a 5-mile trail network suitable for all ages and ability levels. Within the park it's common to spot deer, snapping turtles, and—as you might guess—a variety of birds.
More information: parks.ky.gov/parks/ recreationparks/john-james/default.Aspx

Trail: Mammoth Cave National Park Trail Network
Park: Mammoth Cave National Park
City: Mammoth Cave, Kentucky
Description: With more than 400 miles of underground tunnels already explored, Mammoth Cave is the longest known cave system in the world. But there are more than 80 miles of trail aboveground too, and in recent years they've become very popular with hikers, horseback riders, and mountain bikers alike (though most of the backcountry trails are only for pedestrians and equestrians). Next time

18. Louisiana

Trail: Palmetto, Bayou Coquille, and Marsh Overlook Trails
Park: Jean Lafitte National Historical Park and Preserve—Barataria Preserve
City: Marrero, Louisiana (near New Orleans)
Description: This was one of our favorite hikes of the entire book tour. The 0.9-mile Palmetto Trail is a boardwalk that snakes away from the visitor center through swampland (the word "snakes" is fitting, since we saw dozens of them on this stretch). Then we picked up the 0.5-mile

Bayou Coquille Trail—a boardwalk and packed gravel road—hitting the 0.4-mile Marsh Overlook Trail, where we saw more alligators—from a safe distance—than we'd seen in our combined seventy years. It was pretty incredible—and a little unnerving.

More information: nps.gov/jela/barataria-preserve.htm

Trail: Wild Azalea Trail
Park: Kisatchie National Forest
City: Southwest of Alexandria, Louisiana

Description: The Wild Azalea Trails rolls 28 miles through hardwoods, creeks, and longleaf pines. It's the longest trail in the state and is conveniently located smack in the middle of it. You can hike it year-round, but it can be crazy hot in summer. If you want to see the azaleas in bloom, it's best to go in March or April. The WAT was another happy surprise during our time in Louisiana.

More information: www.fs.usda.gov/recarea/kisatchie/null/recarea/?recid=34655&actid=29

Trail: Lake D'Arbonne Trail Network
Park: Lake D'Arbonne State Park
City: Farmerville, Louisiana

Description: We had a lot of fun exploring some of the shorter hiking trails at Lake D'Arbonne State Park. If you're looking for something longer, check out the White Trail that goes from the visitor center to the lakeshore and back. The park has plenty of recreational activities besides hiking (swimming, fishing, a playground, and bike trails); they have luxury cabins for rent too.

More information: crt.state.la.us/louisiana-state-parks/parks/lake-darbonne-state-park

19. Maine

Trail: French Mountain
Park: Belgrade Regional Conservation Alliance
City: Rome, Maine

Description: They don't call Maine "Vacationland" for nothing. Hiking opportunities abound—so do all other outdoor sports for that matter. Just be sure to bring your bug spray in summer . . . and warm layers the rest of the year. French Mountain is an easy loop that's under 1 mile, so it's perfect for families with young children. It has rewarding views from the summit, which makes for a great picnic spot, and there's usually enough of a breeze to keep those nasty blackflies away.

More information: belgradelakes.org/land/trails/french-mountain

Never mind the body of water—I'm pretty sure the trail goes that way.
DAVIS FAMILY

Trail: Ship Harbor
Park: Acadia National Park
City: Bar Harbor, Maine
Description: We're fudging a little on this one, since we actually did it on our honeymoon, before Charley was around. But she was with us in spirit, so we're going to include it. Acadia is everything they make it out to be. There are dozens of trails to explore, so you should set aside a good three or four days if you go. This 1.3-mile round-trip was probably the most family-friendly hike. It's short, interesting—it passes through conifer forest and along the shoreline—and it makes a figure eight so you can shorten it if you have some tired little puppies on your hands—human or dog. Both are allowed, but the latter must be leashed.
More information: nps.gov/acad/index.htm

Don't be afraid to let 'em get their hands dirty.
MP (MEGAN PETERSON) PHOTOGRAPHY

Trail: Daicey Pond Nature Trail
Park: Baxter State Park
City: Millinocket, Maine
Description: If your kids are in their teens, they might be ready to tackle Mount Katahdin. (Just know that it makes for a long and challenging day and that it shouldn't be attempted if the weather is foul.) But for families with younger kids, the 1.8-mile trail circling Daicey Pond is a less ambitious—and probably wiser—option. The park has a brochure that helps for identifying plants and landmarks along the route. Go early or late in the day and you might even spot a moose!
More information: baxterstatepark authority.com

For more information hiking in Maine, contact the Maine Appalachian Trail Club (matc.org).

20. Maryland

Trail: Appalachian Trail
Park: Pen Mar State Park
City: Washington County, Maryland
Description: Washington County, where Pen Mar is located, claims that the park is "one of the finest scenic areas in Maryland." We're landlubbers and have never been to Maryland's Eastern Shore, so we're inclined to agree. Take an out-and-back along the A.T., let your kids romp around the playground, and enjoy a picnic dinner while soaking in the view. There's even a summer concert series, so bring a blanket and some lawn chairs. Bonus: The park is a stone's throw from Pennsylvania and crosses the Mason-Dixon Line, so if you're ambitious—or even if you're not—you can say your family literally hiked from the South to the North along the A.T.
More information: washco-md.net/parks_facilities/p-PenMarPark.shtm

Long-distance trail: Potomac Heritage National Scenic Trail

Description: One other trail worth mentioning is the 710-mile Potomac Heritage Trail, which spans the entire state of Maryland from Chesapeake Bay in the east to the Allegheny Highlands in the west. The system is still evolving, but you can already hike more than 350 miles of it on trails and sidewalks from Washington, DC, to Seward, Pennsylvania, just east of Pittsburgh. Pretty cool, huh?

More information: nps.gov/pohe/index .htm

For more information on hiking in Maryland, contact the Capital Hiking Club (capitalhikingclub.org/ home.aspx), the Maryland Outdoor Club (maryland outdoorclub.org/), or the Mountain Club of Maryland (mcomd.org).

21. Massachusetts

Trail: Appalachian Trail at Mount Greylock
Park: Mount Greylock State Reservation

Description: Never mind that Mount Greylock is called a "reservation" and not a park—those Massachunutts are something else. We'd be remiss if we didn't include Mount Greylock in this list because, well, we just love it. It's the highest mountain in the Commonwealth of Massachusetts, and one of our all-time favorite hiking quotes is emblazoned on a rock at the summit: "It were as well to be educated in the shadow of a mountain as in more classical shades. Some will remember, no doubt, not only that they went to the college, but that they went to the mountain." Who said it? None other than Henry David Thoreau.

More information: mass.gov/eea/agencies/ dcr/massparks/region-west/mt-greylock -state-reservation-generic.html

Put your kids on your neck if they hit the wall before you finish your hike.
DAVIS FAMILY

Long-distance trail: New England Trail

Description: You may have heard that the Appalachian Trail runs through the Berkshires, but did you know Massachusetts sports a *second* national scenic trail? It's called the New England Trail, and it runs 215 miles from Connecticut's Long Island Sound to the border of New Hampshire, passing cities like Springfield, Holyoke, Amherst, and Warwick in the central part of the state. How do you like them apples?

More information: newenglandtrail.org

For more information on hiking in Massachusetts, contact your local chapter of the Appalachian Mountain Club (outdoors.org)

Wow, now that's a sunset.
DAVIS FAMILY

 22. Michigan

Trail: Sleeping Bear Point and Dunes Trails
Park: Sleeping Bear Dunes National Lakeshore
City: Empire, Michigan
Description: Have we mentioned how much we love Michigan (ahem, in summer)? The water in Lake Michigan is bluer than the Gulf of Mexico, the highs in Traverse City rarely get out of the 70s, and you can literally go cherry picking at dozens of farms. The sandier trails at Sleeping Bear Dunes can be, well, a real bear (especially for the little ones). And you definitely don't want to hike down the steepest dunes to the water unless you're sure you can make it back up. One family-friendly alternative is Windy Moraine, which has berries in season and a lot more shade, making it a nice reprieve on clear summer days. The park has something called the Trekker's Challenge for those who want to hike all 100 miles of trail in a calendar year.
More information: nps.gov/slbe/index .htm

 Trail: Escarpment Trail/Presque Isle River Area
Park: Porcupine Mountain State Park
City: Ontonagon, Michigan
Description: We hiked a couple of trails in the Porkies, and Brew found his happy place amid 10,000 skipping stones on the shore of Lake Superior at sunset. Our two favorite trails were the Escarpment, which provided lovely views off oft-photographed Lake of the Clouds, and the trails at the Presque Isle River campground, which followed the rapids and waterfalls before the river emptied into the lake. If you're fortunate enough to spend time in the Upper Peninsula— or if you call it home—be sure to visit the Porkies. They're just a little shy, but they're plenty friendly.
More information: michigandnr.com/ parksandtrails/details.aspx?type=SPRK &id=426

Trail: The North Country Trail
Description: The North Country Trail meanders through Michigan for hundreds and hundreds of miles. It's headquartered in Lowell outside of Grand Rapids. For more information, visit northcountrytrail .org.

23. Minnesota

 Trail: Minnehaha Falls
Park: Minnehaha Regional Park
City: Minneapolis, Minnesota
Description: This is one of our very favorite urban trail systems. With awesome views of 53-foot Minnehaha Falls and trails above the bluffs and below the falls leading to the banks of the Mississippi River, you'll have plenty of time to work up an appetite and enjoy a Jucy Lucy. (For the uninitiated,

Minneapolitans like to put the cheese inside the meat. Once you try it, you'll never go back.)

More information: minneapolisparks. org/parks__destinations/parks__lakes/ minnehaha_regional_park

Trail: Superior Hiking Trail (Rose Garden to Hartley Nature Center)
Park: Hartley Nature Center
City: Duluth, Minnesota
Description: The Superior Hiking Trail curves 300 miles along—you guessed it—Lake Superior. But there are convenient road crossings and trailheads along the way—including a full 42 miles in and around Duluth—so mellower family outings are possible anywhere. We started at the edge of downtown, where the singletrack followed a creek upstream for a mile or so before reaching the Hartley Nature Center. This was the perfect turnaround spot because there was a creek and playground for Charley to enjoy.

More information: shta.org

In the cliffs near Minnehaha Falls in Minneapolis
DAVIS FAMILY

Don't forget a towel and bathing suits when you hike to the swimming hole!
DAVIS FAMILY

24. Mississippi

Trail: Black Creek Trail
Park: Big Creek Landing Recreation Area
City: Hattiesburg, Mississippi
Description: You don't have to hike the entirety of this 41-mile trail to appreciate its beauty, but after doing a short out-and-back stretch along Cypress Creek at Big Creek Landing, you might decide that you want to.
More information: www.fs.usda.gov/detail/mississippi/about-forest/districts/?cid=stelprdb5209588

Trail: Al Scheller Trail
Park: Vicksburg National Military Park
City: Vicksburg, Mississippi
Description: Jefferson Davis said, "Vicksburg is the nail head that holds the South's two halves together," and Abraham Lincoln said, "Vicksburg is the key." One hundred and fifty years later, the military park there is as hauntingly beautiful as ever. We hiked part of the 12.5-mile Al Scheller Loop Trail as an out-and-back and were surprised by how hilly it was. Come prepared to have a great day of hiking; and come prepared to learn a lot about US history.
More information: nps.gov/vick/index.htm

Long-distance trail: Natchez Trace Trail

Park: Natchez Trace National Scenic Trail

Description: The Natchez Trace Trail stretches 450 miles from Nashville to Natchez, with the majority of it winding its way through Mississippi. Native Americans, pioneers, and traders from Tennessee and Kentucky used the route. So did outlaws and bandits; it was a dangerous but necessary trade corridor. The trail today is deep and dark, full of mystery and rich with history. We hiked the cypress swamp north and west of Jackson, and it made for an excellent day hike.

More information: nps.gov/natt/index .htm

25. Missouri

Trail: MKT Nature and Fitness Trail

Park: Columbia Parks and Recreation

City: Columbia, Missouri

Description: We hiked and ran on the Katy Trail several times during our stay in Columbia. This 238-mile multiuse trail was built on the old railroad bed of the Missouri-Kansas-Texas (MKT) Railroad, so it makes for some flat, easy hiking. Even our brief forays onto it led us past rock cliffs, over muddy creeks, and through meadows with wildflowers bursting into bloom. It was a peaceful escape from the college-town hustle and bustle and one of the real highlights of our time in Missouri.

More information: como.gov/ ParksandRec/Parks/MKT_Trail

Long-distance trail: Ozark Trail
Park: Mark Twain National Forest

Description: Rumor has it that when you hike through Mark Twain National Forest on this 400-mile trail, you instantly become funnier and a better writer. We should go there sometime. Eventually the trail will wind its way from St. Louis to the border of Arkansas, where it will meet up with the Ozark Highlands Trail to make possible a 700-mile thru-hike. So far there's a stretch of 230 miles in Missouri that intrepid thru-hikers have been undertaking. The trail was dreamed up in 1977, and the two organizations that watch over the trail—the Ozark Trail Association and Ozark Trail Council—have made great strides in building and connecting single-track in recent years.

More information: ozarktrail.com/index .php

Charley keeping cool on an urban hike in Ohio
DAVIS FAMILY

26. Montana

Trail: Prairie Trail
Park: Mount Helena City Park
City: Helena, Montana
Description: Helena has more than 75 miles of hiking trails, and Mount Helena City Park, which borders the downtown business district, is a perfect place for a short hike with the family. We stuck with the Prairie Trail because the wildflowers were out and it was flatter and easier for Charley to manage. The views of the city and the valley beyond are impressive, and there are dozens of restaurants (and a brewery—Brew insisted we mention the brewery) just seconds away once you've worked up an appetite.
More information: visitmt.com/listings/general/city-park/mount-helena-city-park.html

Trail: Trail of the Cedars
Park: Glacier National Park
City: West Glacier, Montana
Description: Glacier is a national treasure, and there are entire guide-books about the park's more than 700 miles of hiking trails. Families with more experience and ambition may want to start with the stunning 7.6-mile (one-way) Highline Trail to Granite Park Chalet. For families with younger children or who need wheelchair accessibility, the Trail of the Cedars is a good choice. This hike packs a lot into a 1-mile loop—hundred-foot cedars, views of Avalanche Gorge and powerful Avalanche Creek, and markers identifying flora and fauna along the way.
More information: nps.gov/glac/index.htm

Ice on a winter day in the southern Appalachians
DAVIS FAMILY

Long-distance trail: Pacific Northwest Trail

Description: The spectacular Pacific Northwest Trail stretches 1,200 miles from the Continental Divide to the Pacific Ocean and passes through national parks, national wilderness, and numerous trail towns along the way. Together with the Continental Divide Trail, the Grand Enchantment Trail, the Arizona Trail, and the Pacific Crest Trail, it forms a 6,785-mile "trail nirvana" known as the Great Western Loop. So that's something to work up to as a family.

More information: pnt.org

For more information on hiking in Montana, contact the Sierra Club Montana Chapter (montana.sierra club.org) or any number of trail groups in Billings, Bozeman, Butte, Big Sky; the list goes on (and is not exclusive to towns beginning with the letter "B").

Green, green, and more green
DAVIS FAMILY

27. Nebraska

Trail: Meadowlark and North Island Trails
Park: Boyer Chute National Wildlife
City: Fort Calhoun, Nebraska
Description: We hiked here on our way into Omaha because we wanted to see what a Missouri River floodplain looks like. The trails were easy and flat, so they were perfect for Charley. It's also an exceptional spot for viewing migratory waterfowl. We had the place entirely to ourselves for the 2 hours or so we were there.
More information: fws.gov/refuge/boyer_chute

Trail: Kearney Hike and Bike Trail
Park: Cottonmill Park
City: Kearney, Nebraska
Description: Kearney is a cute little college town on the plains of central Nebraska. We made two stops there on book tour and enjoyed walking along the city's 13-mile paved Hike and Bike Trail while there. More trains pass through Nebraska than anywhere else in the country, so it's no wonder "rails to trails" abound. If you call this region home, chances are you're very close to some great walking routes—and some outstanding opportunities for birding.
More information: traillink.com/trail/kearney-hike-and-bike-trail.aspx

28. Nevada

Trail: Rainbow Vista Trail
Park: Valley of Fire State Park
City: Moapa Valley, Nevada
Description: Valley of Fire is a hidden gem outside Las Vegas with a plethora of hiking trails. The Rainbow Vista path is one of the most beautiful and family-friendly. Your kids will enjoy digging in the desert sand, and you'll enjoy the stunning views and polychrome rock cliffs. As you leave the park, check

Best . . . sandbox . . . ever!
DAVIS FAMILY

Appalachian Trail before meandering through a series of rock ledges. Its length and moderate elevation change make it a good stepping-stone if you're building up toward more ambitious day hikes or something really big, like a Presidential Traverse in the White Mountains.
More information: outdoors.dartmouth .edu/activities/hiking/hikes/velvetrocks .html

For more information on hiking in New Hampshire, contact the New Hampshire chapter of the Appalachian Mountain Club (amc-nh.org/index .php), the Dartmouth Outing Club (outdoors .dartmouth.edu/doc), or the Randolph Mountain Club (randolphmountainclub.org).

30. New Jersey

Trail: Monument Trail
Park: High Point State Park
City: Sussex, New Jersey
Description: High Point State Park has more than 50 miles of trails. This 3.7-mile loop takes you to the highest point in New Jersey, with great views of the Delaware River and the surrounding landscape. On a clear day, from the base of the monument you can see a sizable portion of three states: New Jersey, New York, and Pennsylvania.
More information: www.state.nj.us/dep/ parksandforests/parks/highpoint.html

To find out more about hiking in the Garden State, contact the New York–New Jersey Trail Conference at nynjtc.org.

out the petroglyphs at the nearby Mouse Trap Trail.
More information: parks.nv.gov/parks/ valley-of-fire-state-park

29. New Hampshire

Trail: Velvet Rocks
Park: Appalachian Trail
City: Hanover, New Hampshire
Description: This 5.2-mile round-trip starts in Hanover and follows the

31. New Mexico

Trail: Bear Canyon Trail
Park: Randall Davey Audubon Center
City: Santa Fe, New Mexico
Description: The 1.5-mile Bear Canyon Trail at the Randall Davey Audubon Center lets kids explore a side canyon

while offering shade and intriguing rock formations before the grade becomes too steep to climb. At the moment, the garden is the only part of the park that is accessible to wheelchairs, but they plan to make significant modifications to the trail system by the end of 2017.
More information: nm.audubon.org/ randall-davey-audubon-center -sanctuary

Long-distance trail: Grand Enchantment Trail
Description: The Grand Enchantment Trail travels 770 miles and crosses fourteen mountain ranges on its way from Phoenix to Albuquerque. About 60 percent of it is singletrack at this time. Only around since 2003, the trail has already become one of the most popular long-distance trails in the country.
More information: simblissity.net/ get-about.shtml

32. New York

Trail: Niagara Gorge Rim Trail
Park: Niagara Falls State Park
City: Niagara Falls, New York
Description: This 6.2-mile one-way hike was one of the very first we took on our book tour. And after being surrounded by the masses at the falls themselves, we really appreciated this trail's relative seclusion. It requires a shuttle but is well worth the logistical effort as it follows the Niagara River downstream and passes impressive features like "The Whirlpool" and "Devil's Hole Rapids." The trail is fairly level and also offers a good amount of shade.
More information: niagarafallsstatepark .com

Charley and her friend Max on a hike in New Hampshire
DAVIS FAMILY

Trail: Pitchoff Mountain
Park: The Adirondack Park
City: Keene, New York
Description: We hiked this 3.1-mile round-trip near Cascade Lake and had a picnic lunch at the summit while taking in the mesmerizing 360-degree views. A relatively gradual climb, the trail became a bit steeper toward the top, when our legs were really begging for a break.
More Information: apa.ny.gov/about_park

For more information on hiking in New York, contact the New York–New Jersey Trail Conference (nynjtc .org), the Adirondack Mountain Club (adk.org), or the Catskill Mountain Club (catskillmountainclub .org/events).

Red eft in the Appalachians in spring
DAVIS FAMILY

National Park to Jockey's Ridge State Park on the Atlantic Ocean. It's a magnificent variety of mountains, foothills, and coastal wetlands, and it passes close to most of the major cities the state.
More information: ncmst.org

For more information on hiking in North Carolina, contact the Carolina Mountain Club (carolina mountainclub.org).

33. North Carolina

Trail: Balsam Nature Trail
Park: Mount Mitchell State Park
City: Burnsville, North Carolina
Description: This 0.75-mile hike allows you to experience the spruce-fir forest that crowns the summit of Mount Mitchell. At 6,684 feet in elevation, it's the highest peak east of the Mississippi River. If you're looking for more of a challenge, use the Old Mitchell or Commissary Trail to reach the top.
More information: ncparks.gov/mount-mitchell-state-park

Long-distance trail: Mountains-to-Sea Trail
Description: North Carolina's Mountains-to-Sea Trail stretches 1,150 miles from Great Smoky Mountains

34. North Dakota

Trail: Hay Creek Trail (near Pebble Creek Golf Course)
Park: North Dakota Parks and Recreation
City: Bismarck, North Dakota
Description: We had been told by locals to check out Fort Abraham Lincoln State Park on the other side of the Missouri River in Mandan. But we thought better of keeping Charley out in some nasty weather and took a stroll on the Hay Creek Trail instead. And you know what? It was terrific.
More information: parkrec.nd.gov/activities/national_recreation/hay_creek.html

Long-distance trail: Maah Daah Hey Trail
Description: The Maah Daah Hey Trail Association says this is "North Dakota's Best Kept Secret." We would say it's one of the *country's* best kept secrets (at least until our book becomes a bestseller). This 97-mile trail (whose name means "an area that has been or will be around for a long time") abounds with wildlife like mule deer, bighorn sheep, elk, prairie dogs, wild turkeys, birds of prey, even the occasional mountain lion, and is open to hikers and mountain bikers alike.
More information: mdhta.com

35. Ohio

Trail: West and East Cohasset Trails
Park: Mill Creek Metro Park
City: Youngstown, Ohio
Description: We were really impressed with this city park in Youngstown. We explored several areas, but probably our favorite trail was a 2.8-mile loop we made by combining the West Cohasset Trail, which passes beneath mature hemlocks, and the East, which crosses a fun suspension bridge.
More information: millcreekmetroparks.org/visit/hiking

Trail: Brandywine Gorge Loop
Park: Cuyahoga Valley National Park
City: Brecksville, Ohio
Description: This 1.5-mile hike has lovely views of Brandywine Creek and passes underneath shale and sandstone rock formations. The short out-and-back to the Brandywine Falls viewing platform is definitely worth it.
More information: nps.gov/cuva/index.htm

Long-distance trail: Buckeye Trail
Description: The Buckeye Trail is 1,444 miles long and makes a giant circle around the state. If you're an Ohioan, there's a good chance you're not more than an hour's drive from a trailhead. Hikers we've met from Ohio are extremely proud of their state trail. And the Buckeye Trail Association is doing a fantastic job of maintaining and promoting it.
More information: buckeyetrail.org

For more information on hiking in Ohio, contact the Buckeye Trail Association (buckeyetrail.org).

36. Oklahoma

Trail: Martin Park Nature Trails
Park: Martin Park Nature Center
City: Oklahoma City, Oklahoma
Description: The Martin Park Nature Center has 2.5 miles of trails, and we enjoyed exploring most of them during our stay in OKC. Completed in 2015, the 1.5-mile Wilderness Matters INTEGRIS Jim Thorpe Courage Trail is designed to accommodate people with differences. In 2017 the park plans to enhance the trail by adding touch-based interpretive exhibits with Braille and a wheelchair-accessible tree house.
More information: okc.gov/recreation/martin-nature-park

Long-distance trail: Ouachita National Recreation Trail
Description: We mentioned the Ouachita Trail in the section on Arkansas, but a sizable portion lies in eastern Oklahoma. You can find maps and a comprehensive description from the USDA Forest Service at www.fs.usda.gov/Internet/FSE_DOCUMENTS/fsm9_039448.pdf
More information: friendsot.org

We made it to the top and we are all rock stars!
MARY ROUX

37. Oregon

Trail: Wildwood Trail
Park: Forest Park
City: Portland, Oregon
Description: Forest Park sits on the west side of Portland and is the largest urban forest in the country. It boasts the 40-mile Wildwood Trail as well as some impressive old-growth forests and is an amazing resource for Portlanders.
More information: forestpark conservancy.org/forest-park

Trail: Benham Falls (Deschutes River Trail)
Park: Deschutes National Forest
City: Bend, Oregon
Description: As with so many towns out west, the hiking options in Bend are a bit overwhelming. Fortunately, we have friends in town who have two young boys, so they're well versed in family-friendly hikes. They took us to the Benham Falls West Day Use Area, where the path was smooth and the waterfalls along the Deschutes River were impressive.
More information: www.fs.usda.gov/recarea/deschutes/recarea/?recid=38292

Long-distance trail: Oregon Coast Trail
Description: The first time we saw the Oregon coastline, we were blown away by its beauty, so we can only imagine how amazing the 382-mile Oregon Coast Trail must be. For the most part it follows the beach, but it also crosses through state parks, public lands, and private property. It runs the entire length of the state and is broken down into northern, central, and southern sections.
More information: oregon.gov/oprd/parks/Pages/oct_main.aspx

For more information on hiking in Oregon, contact Trailkeepers of Oregon (trailkeepersoforegon.org).

38. Pennsylvania

Trail: Valley Creek Trail
Park: Valley Forge National Historical Park
City: Tredyffrin Township, Pennsylvania (near Philadelphia)
Description: This quiet 1.5-mile path starts at Washington's Headquarters on the Schuylkill River and meanders along a scenic creek. The trail is well graded and

appropriate for youngsters. If you want more of a challenge, combine this path with the Mount Misery Trail (if you dare) to gain some elevation and make a loop.
More information: nps.gov/vafo/index.htm

Trail: The Appalachian Trail at Pine Grove Furnace
Park: Pine Grove Furnace State Park
City: Gardners, Pennsylvania
Description: This hike features the Appalachian Trail Museum, the A.T.'s traditional halfway point, a cold lake for swimming, and some great views. Follow the trail to the Pole Steeple Overlook then take the Pole Steeple Trail to Laurel Lake and connect back to Pine Grove Furnace along the Mountain Creek Trail for a 3.5-miler.
More information: dcnr.state.pa.us/stateparks/findapark/pinegrovefurnace/index.htm

Long-distance trail: Loyalsock Trail
Description: We've heard great things about this 59-mile trail, which travels through the Loyalsock State Forest in north central Pennsylvania. It follows Loyalsock Creek through dense hardwood forest, has some outstanding views, and has been maintained by The Alpine Club of Williamsport since 1953.
More information: lycoming.org/alpine

For more information on hiking in Pennsylvania, contact one of the following:
Keystone Trails Association (kta-hike.org/index.php)
Blue Mountain Eagle Climbing Club (bmecc.org)
Allentown Hiking Club (allentownhikingclub.org)
Susquehanna Appalachian Trail Club (satc-hike.org)
York Hiking Club (yorkhikingclub.com)
Cumberland Valley Appalachian Trail Club (cvatclub.org)

Hiker logo on the Appalachian Trail
DAVIS FAMILY

39. Rhode Island

Trail: Clay Head Trail
Park: Clay Head Preserve
City: Block Island, Rhode Island
Description: The pristine beaches, impressive views, clay bluffs, and migratory songbirds on this privately owned 150-acre preserve make the 2-mile hike here a must for Rhode Islanders. Your kids will also enjoy exploring "the maze," a network of unnamed, unmarked grass trails farther removed from the coastline.
More information: nature.org/our initiatives/regions/northamerica/united states/rhodeisland/placesweprotect/clay-head-preserve.xml

40. South Carolina

Trail: Carrick Creek Trail
Park: Table Rock State Park
City: Pickens, South Carolina
Description: This 2-mile loop will lead you past a cascading steam and into

a mixed hardwood forest filled with rho-dodendron and mountain laurel. It also offers some great views of Table Rock State Park, especially in winter.
More information: southcarolinaparks.com/tablerock/introduction.aspx

Long-distance trail: Foothills Trail
Description: The Foothills Trail runs 77 miles through the Upstate (westernmost South Carolina) from Table Rock State Park to Oconee State Park. As it winds along the Escarpment, it passes an abundance of waterfalls and has a surprising amount of elevation gain and loss. This is an outstanding long-distance hike by any standard and makes for excellent day hiking as well.
More information: foothillstrail.org

Long-distance trail: Palmetto Trail
Description: The Palmetto Trail will eventually wind 500 miles from the foothills to the coast. Three hundred fifty miles of the trail are already completed, and since it more or less cuts the state in half, South

Carolinians are rarely more than a 2-hour drive from it.
More information: palmettoconservation.org

41. South Dakota

Trail: Horsethief Lake Trail
Park: Black Hills National Forest
City: Mount Rushmore, South Dakota
Description: This 2.7-mile loop meanders through forest and along the shoreline near Horsethief Lake Campground. It's a great place to escape the crowds at Mount Rushmore and find some solitude in Black Hills National Forest.
More information: www.fs.usda.gov/blackhills

Trail: Falls of the Big Sioux River
Park: Falls Park
City: Sioux Falls, South Dakota
Description: We really enjoyed exploring the paved pathways around the falls for which Sioux Falls is named.

Badlands National Park, South Dakota
DAVIS FAMILY

The park has an observation tower and multiple viewing platforms by the water's edge. If you really want to have your socks knocked off, visit from mid-November to early January for the annual Winter Wonderland.
More information: visitsiouxfalls.com/things-to-do/falls-park

Long-distance trail: Centennial Trail
Description: The Centennial Trail starts at Bear Butte (a sacred space to Native Americans) in the north and cuts through Black Hills National Forest and past Mount Rushmore before reaching its southern terminus 111 miles later at Wind Cave National Park. We enjoyed hiking on it briefly during our visit to South Dakota and hope to return someday to cross it off our bucket list.
More information: www.fs.usda.gov/Internet/FSE_DOCUMENTS/stelprdb5194547.pdf

42. Tennessee

Trail: White and Red Trails
Park: Percy Warner Park
City: Nashville, Tennessee
Description: This urban park has a fantastic trail system and makes you feel as though you're in the middle of nowhere, even though you're only 9 miles from downtown. The 2.5-mile White Trail offers solid climbs and accompanying views in every direction; the Red Trail, which makes a figure eight with the White Trail, is another 4.5 miles long. You can take the connector trail to Edwin Warner Park to access another 5 miles of singletrack.
More information: nashville.gov/Parks-and-Recreation/Parks/Warner-Parks.aspx

Sometimes it's best to take it nice and slow.
DAVIS FAMILY

Trail: Walls of Jericho
Park: Walls of Jericho State Natural Area
City: Tennessee-Alabama border
Description: This 7-mile out-and-back straddles the border with Alabama at the southern end of the Cumberland Plateau. The Nature Conservancy fought hard to preserve this spot, and for good reason. The sheer rock walls create an impressive amphitheater around the headwaters of the Paint Rock River.
More information: backpacker.com/trips/tennessee/chattanooga/chattanooga-tn-walls-of-jericho

Trail: Yellow, White, and Blue Trails
Parks: Shelby Farms Park
City: Memphis, Tennessee
Description: Shelby Farms Park is one of the largest urban parks in the country and has miles of singletrack to explore along the Wolf River. The park also has a "Discovery Playground" and adjoins the Wolf River Greenway, a

5-mile-long path of crushed limestone and asphalt that passes through forest and reclaimed farmland.
More information: shelbyfarmspark.org; wolfriver.org

Long-distance trail: Cumberland Trail
Description: The 300-mile Cumberland Trail travels along the Cumberland Plateau from Chickamauga and Chattanooga National Military Park in the south to Cumberland Gap National Historical Park in the north. It's part of the Great Eastern Trail and is maintained by the Cumberland Trails Conference.
More information: cumberlandtrail.org

Enchanted Rock
©ISTOCK.COM/DEAN_FIKAR

43. Texas

Trail: Summit Trail
Park: Enchanted Rock State Natural Area
City: Fredericksburg, Texas
Description: Often referred to as the Ayers Rock of Texas, Enchanted Rock is a giant granite batholith—basically, a giant volcanic rock—that rises above the Hill Country to create a stunning natural landmark and a great place to hike. Most of the trails here are family-friendly (so long as you're used to the sweltering summer heat), but the 1.6-mile Summit Trail will take you to the top of the rock and provide the best views.
More information: tpwd.texas.gov/ state-parks/enchanted-rock

Long-distance trail: Lone Star Hiking Trail
Description: An hour or so north of Houston and 4 hours from Dallas is the Lone Star Hiking Trail, a 144-mile jaunt through the hardwoods, pines, and creeks of Sam Houston National Forest. The landscape is flat and the tread is smooth, so this makes for some terrific beginner-friendly hiking. If you live in the eastern half of the state—or even if you don't—it would be well worth your time to check this trail out.
More information: lonestartrail.org

For more information on hiking in Texas, contact the Lone Star Hiking Club (lonestartrail.org)

44. Utah

Trail: Riverside Walk
Park: Zion National Park
City: Springdale, Utah
Description: This easy 2-mile out-and-back leads hikers along the Virgin River to the famous "Narrows." It's doubtful your crew will want to slog upstream to

explore all 16 miles of canyon, but they'll enjoy splashing in the water for a bit, and you can turn around whenever you want. The Narrows are very popular, so try to go early or late in the day or outside of tourist season (late spring and summer). Also, if anyone sees a blue stuffed seal, please contact us. Answering to the name "Harpie," he fell out of Charley's kid pack during our visit.

More information: nps.gov/zion/index .htm

Trail: Queens Garden
Park: Bryce Canyon National Park
City: Bryce, Utah
Description: This gentle 1.8-mile hike will get you into the canyon and near the hoodoos and rock formations that make Bryce so appealing. There's

some elevation gain and loss, since you descend from the rim. But the striking scenery demands that you take photos, so you'll have plenty of excuses to stop and catch your breath.

More information: nps.gov/brca/index .htm

For more information on hiking in Utah, contact the Wasatch Mountain Club (wasatchmountainclub .org).

45. Vermont

Trail: South Shore Trail
Park: Willoughby State Forest
City: Sutton, Vermont
Description: This pleasant 1-mile stroll follows the shore of Lake Willoughby and is appropriate for children of all ages. If you have older or more

A tight squeeze on the Appalachian Trail
DAVIS FAMILY

hike will bring you to Mountain Meadow Lodge, where you can turn around, enjoy a meal, or even spend the night. The lodge serves up some tasty dishes—they also have a pet pig!
More information: vtstateparks.com/htm/gifford.htm

Long-distance trail: The Long Trail
Description: Vermont's 272-mile Long Trail is the oldest long-distance trail in the country. It follows the Green Mountains from the Massachusetts border all the way to Canada and can be accessed for day hikes at dozens of road crossings and trailheads throughout the state.
More information: greenmountainclub.org/the-long-trail

For more information on hiking in Vermont, contact the Green Mountain Club (greenmountainclub.org).

46. Virginia

Trail: Osprey and Kingfisher Trails
Park: First Landing State Park
City: Virginia Beach, Virginia
Description: English colonists landed here more than 400 years ago and today First Landing State Park is an oasis of trails, forests and swampland in the Tidewater region that boasts dozens of miles of single track and some of the best bird watching in Virginia.

For more information on hiking in Virginia, contact one of these trail clubs:
Old Dominion Appalachian Trail Club (olddominiontrailclub.onefireplace.org)
Tidewater Appalachian Trail Club (tidewateratc.com)
Natural Bridge Appalachian Trail Club (nbatc.org)
Outdoor Club at Virginia Tech (www.outdoor.org.vt.edu)
Roanoke Appalachian Trail Club (ratc.org)
Piedmont Appalachian Trail Hikers (path-at.org)
Mount Rogers Appalachian Trail Club (mratc.pbworks.com/w/page/8862374/FrontPage)

advanced hikers, check out one of the nearby trails to the summit of Mount Pisgah.
More information: vtstateparks.com/pdfs/willoughbystateforest.pdf

Trail: The Appalachian Trail at Kent Pond
Park: Gifford Woods State Park
City: Killington, Vermont
Description: Start your day by enjoying the amenities at Gifford Woods then take the Appalachian Trail out of the park and across VT 100, where you can explore the shoreline of scenic Kent Pond. A 1-mile

47. Washington

Trail: Skyline Trail
Park: Badger Mountain
City: Richland, Washington
Description: With 7 miles of trail and counting, Badger Mountain is a hiker's oasis in the heart of Washington wine country. For outstanding views of the region, take an out-and-back on the 2.9-mile Skyline Trail. And if the kids wear you out on the hike, be sure to pick up a bottle (or a case) of Cabernet, Merlot, or Petit Verdot.
More information: friendsofbadger.org

For more information on hiking in Washington, contact the Washington Trail Association (wta.org)

48. Washington, DC

Trail: Western Ridge and Valley Trails
Park: Rock Creek Park
City: Washington, DC
Description: Two trails—the Western Ridge and the Valley—flank Rock Creek and offer miles of hiking and endless route options in our nation's capital. There are also picnic tables; the only planetarium in the entire national park system; and a nature center with a Discovery Room, live turtles, snakes, and an active beehive. Not bad for a metro area with six million people, eh?
More information: nps.gov/rocr/index .htm

For more information on hiking in Washington, DC, contact the Capital Hiking Club (capitalhikingclub .org/home.aspx).

49. West Virginia

Trail: Rocky Ridge Trail
Park: Kanawha State Forest
City: Charleston, West Virginia
Description: As the name implies,

this beautiful 2-mile path has some steep sections but overall isn't too difficult. You can combine it with the Pigeon Roost Trail to make a loop, and there are a couple of playgrounds and a picnic area near the trailhead.
More information: kanawhastateforest .com

For more information on hiking in West Virginia, contact the Kanawha Trail Club (kanawhatrailclub .org).

50. Wisconsin

Trail: Ice Age Trail to Stone Elephant
Park: Kettle Moraine
City: 37 miles southwest of Milwaukee, Wisconsin (61 miles east of Madison)
Description: We did a 4-mile out-and-back on the Ice Age Trail to the Stone Elephant through lovely meadows and hardwood forests. Much of the trail follows the escarpment and offers views of the flatlands below. The Stone Elephant

Craggy Pinnacle sunset, North Carolina
DAVIS FAMILY

was much smaller than we expected. Also, we think it should be called "Stone Woolly Mammoth," since that's the symbol for the Ice Age Trail.
More information: dnr.wi.gov/topic/parks/name/kms

Long-distance trail: Ice Age National Scenic Trail
Description: The 1,200-mile Ice Age Trail twists and turns across Wisconsin, passing through thirty-one counties along the way. The name comes from the most recent ice age, more than 12,000 years ago, which formed the landscape the trail intersects. More than one million people use the trail each year, and a dedicated group of volunteers maintain the trail under the guidance of the Ice Age Trail Alliance.
More information: iceagetrail.org

For more information on hiking in Wisconsin, contact the Ice Age Trail Alliance (iceagetrail.org).

51. Wyoming

Trail: Canyon Trail
Park: Sinks Canyon State Park
City: Lander, Wyoming
Description: Sinks Canyon State Park at the southeast edge of the Wind River Range is named for a bizarre spot on the Popo Agie River where the waters disappear underground only to resurface a quarter-mile later. Even more intriguing is the fact that dye tests have proven the water takes more than 2 hours to travel that quarter-mile. The 4-mile Canyon Trail above the Sinks gains some solid elevation and offers terrific views back down the canyon toward Lander.
More information: sinkscanyonstate park.org

Trail: Cache Creek Trail
Park: Trail and Pathways (Teton County Parks and Recreation)
City: Jackson, Wyoming

Rocky walls and rocky trails
KAREN RIDDLE

Description: The Jackson area has some seriously epic hiking trails (not the least of which is the 13-mile Grand Traverse through the Tetons). But if you're looking for something a little less epic and a little closer, the 2.5-mile Cache Creek Trail on the east edge of town fits the bill. The trail gains 850 feet, but it's gradual; and since it's an out-and-back, you can flip it whenever you want.

More information: tetonparksandrec.org/parks-pathways/winter-trail-grooming/trail-pathway-descriptions

The pot of gold's all around you—can't you see it?
MP (MEGAN PETERSON) PHOTOGRAPHY

Index

Hiking back from Kaena Point, the westernmost tip of Oahu
DAVIS FAMILY

Sunset in the Sierras
DAVIS FAMILY

72; conservation and, 132; environment and, 131–32; fire-building and, 73; first-aid skills and, 36; footwear, 55; gear for, 55, 57; GPS and, 91; independent study and, 73; internship of, 132, 133; Leave No Trace ethics and, 131, 133; medical emergencies and, 37; music and, 108; "riff-off" and, 108; self-image of, 70; skills, 89–91; social groups, 37; social media and , 36; survival skills, 108; trail etiquette and, 131; volunteering, 132–33

"hike your own hike," xix, 63

hiking poles, 90, 91, 140, 144; amputees and, 159; blind hikers and, 162; cerebral palsy hikers and, 165; children's and, 48; Down syndrome hikers and, 172

Hitchcock Nature Center, 190

Hoffarth, Stephanie, 109

Homemade Beef Jerky, 88

Honolulu Watershed Forest Reserve, 187–88

Hoosier Hikers Council, 190

Horsethief Lake Campground, 208

Horsethief Lake Trail, SD, 208

Housatonic River Walk, 186

Howler whistle, 85

hydration system, 48

HYOH. See "hike your own hike."

hyperthermia, 27

hypoglycemia, 171

hyponatremia, 28

hypothermia, 42

I Spy game, 95

iBird app, 77

Ice Age National Scenic Trail, WI, 214

Ice Age Trail Alliance, 214

Ice Age Trail to Stone Elephant, WI, 213–14

Idaho Centennial Trail, ID, 188

Idaho trails, 133, 188

Illinois trails, 189

iNaturalist app, 129

Indian Fort Mountain Trail, KY, 191

Indiana Dunes National Lakeshore, 189

Indiana trails, 181, 189–90

inexperience, overcoming, 2

insect spray, 192

instincts, 15; safety and, 10

insulin, 170, 171

Iowa trails, 190–91

Jean Lafitte National Historical Park and Preserve, LA, 125, 192–93

Jester Park, IA, 190

JetScream whistle, 85

Jim Thorpe Courage Trail, OK, 205

Jockey's Ridge State Park, 204

John Hunter Memorial Trail, AK, 182

John James Audubon State Park, 192

John James Audubon Trails, KY, 192

John Muir Trail, CA, 185

junior ranger programs, 68

Kain, Chris, 166–67, 168–69

Kain, Kellisa, 148, 166–67, 168–69

Kanawha State Forest, 213

Kanawha Trail Club, 213

Kansas trails, 191

Katy Trail, MO, 199

Kearney Hike and Bike Trail, NE, 201

Kent Pond, VT, 212

Kentucky trails, 191–92

Kettle Moraine, 213

Keystone Trails Association, 207

Kingfisher Trail, VA, 212

Kinsella, Ken, xxv

Kisatchie National Forest, 193

knife: as hiking tool, 42; skills, 87

knot tying, 87

Know Your State game, 97

Konza Prairie Biological Station, 191

Kozel, Stacey, 157

kudza, invasive plant, 131

Kuo, Frances , 156–57

La Chua Trail, FL, 187

Ladybug Trail, CA, 130

Lake D'Arbonne State Park, 193

Lake D'Arbonne Trail Network, LA, 193

Lake James, IN, 190

Lake Michigan, 196

Lake Superior, 196, 197

Lake Trail, TN, 135

Lake Willoughby, 211

Last Child in the Woods, 73

latrine, woodland, 35

Lawrence Mountain Bike Trail, KS, 191

Lawrence Riverfront Park, 191

Leave No Trace, 117, 119; certification, 133; high school hikers and, 131, 133; preschool hikers and, 125; principles, xxi, 8, 121

Lepore, Roni, 161

letterboxing game, 103, 105

lifesaving. See safety.

lighting, 26–27

"lighting position," 27

Lincoln, Abraham, 198

Little Grand Canyon Trail, IL, 189

local parks, 5

Lone Star Hiking Trail, TX, 210

Long Trail, VT, 137, 212

long-distance trails: Buckeye Trail, 205; Centennial Trail, 209; Colorado Trail, 186; Cumberland Trail, 210; Florida National Scenic Trail, 187; Foothills Trail, 208; Grand Enchantment Trail, 203; Ice Age National Scenic Trail, 214; Idaho Centennial Trail, 189; John Muir Trail, 185; Lone Star Hiking Trail, 210; Long Trail,

Wyoming waters, smooth as glass
MP (MEGAN PETERSON)
PHOTOGRAPHY

*Never mind the rain dance—let's
do a leaf dance!*
DAVIS FAMILY

Sweeping views in Rocky Mountain National Park, Colorado
SHARON BRODIN

About the Authors

Jennifer Pharr Davis is the founder of Blue Ridge Hiking Company, as well as a long-distance hiker, author, speaker, and ambassador for American Hiking Society. She has hiked more than 13,000 miles on six different continents, including thru-hikes on the Pacific Coast Trail, the Appalachian Trail, the Colorado Trail, the Long Trail, and more. In 2011 she set the unofficial record for the fastest thru-hike of the Appalachian Trail, with a time of 46 days, 11 hours, and 20 minutes—and held this until July 2015. Her adventures have been featured in the *New York Times*, the *Washington Post*, and *Outside* magazine, to name a few. Jennifer has been named Blue Ridge Outdoors Person of the Year and a National Geographic Adventurer of the Year. She's on the Appalachian Trail Conservancy's board and serves as an American Hiking Society ambassador.

Brew Davis works with his wife, Jen, at Blue Ridge Hiking Company. He has hiked in all 50 states, completed numerous ultramarathons (including a 100-miler), and thru-hiked trails across the US and Europe. But his proudest hiking accomplishment is coaxing, prodding, cajoling, and carrying his daughter 6 miles up Mount LeConte last spring in Great Smoky Mountains National Park.